The Complete Coach:
A Brit and a Texan Solve the Coaching Puzzle

Tim Bainton and Jeremy Carl

The Complete Coach:
A Brit and a Texan Solve the Coaching Puzzle

Copyright © 2018 Tim Bainton & Jeremy Carl
ALL RIGHTS RESERVED

No part of this publication may be reproduced, stored in or introduced into a retrieval system, or transmitted, in any form or by any means (electronically, mechanical, photocopying, recording or otherwise), without the prior written permission of both the copyright owners and the publisher of this book.

Re-selling through electronic outlets like (Amazon, Barnes & Noble or eBay) without permission of the publisher is illegal and punishable by law.

The scanning, uploading and distribution of this book via the Internet or via any other means without the permission of the publisher is illegal and punishable by law.

Please purchase only authorized editions and do not participate in or encourage electronic piracy of copyrighted materials.

Your support of the authors' right is appreciated.

ISBN-13: 978-1978041165   ISBN-10: 1978041160

COVER DESIGN AND LAYOUT: HELEN BAINTON

LIBRARY OF CONGRESS CATALOGING-IN-PUBLICATION DATA

Bainton, Tim and Carl, Jeremy
The Complete Coach: A Brit and a Texan Solve the Coaching Puzzle

1. Best Practices for Coaching in general. 2. Tennis Coaching in particular. 3. Building a Business and a team. 4. Mentoring for Life.
I. Title.

Dedication

We would like to dedicate this book to all the coaches trying to make a difference in someone's life both on and off the court.

"To be a coach is to have a lasting influence on someone, a gift that should be cherished and never taken for granted."
Tim Bainton and Jeremy Carl

A Special Thank You

Jeremy offers thanks to "Melissa, my wonderful and caring wife, and my beautiful daughter, Maggie—the most supportive and loving wife and daughter a husband and father could ever ask for; to my parents and my brother who have always been there to encourage my passions and dreams; to the coaches who guided me as a player and competitor: David Redding, Jack Newman, Tim Siegel, Bobby McKee; and coaching mentors who always modeled for me what it means to be a good coach: Feisal Hassan and Mel Labat."

Tim offers thanks to "my parents for their selfless support of my tennis, my sister for always pushing me to be better; my Uncle John for his guidance and unconditional friendship. Paul Fisher for giving me the opportunity for coaching; Van Metre Companies for taking a risk and supporting my vision; and lastly, my beautiful and talented wife Helen who each day demands that I respect myself and show humility and kindness to the best of my abilities."

Table of Contents

Acknowledgements	7

Warming Up

Introduction	11
Jeremy's Journey	14
Tim's Tale	19

Point 1—First Serve: Three Foundations of Coaching

15 Love – 15 Reasons to be a Coach	23
30 Love – 30 Skills Every Coach Needs	29
40 Love – 40 Goals Coaches Should Try To Attain	35

Point 2—Coaching Fundamentals

5 Building Blocks	46
Chameleon Coach	50
Creating Passionate Problem Solvers on the Court	54
Four Foci of Student Retention	57
Keys to Coaching Champions	60
Mental Metrics for Evaluating Players	64
The Perfect Lesson	80

Point 3—Tennis Management and Leadership

Creating a Successful Program	85
Growing and Developing Your Staff	90
Providing Opportunities	96

Point 4—Tennis as a Business

Collaborations—Working as a Team	101
Tennis Entrepreneurship	106
Tracking Trends and Increasing Profits	110

Point 5—Family Values
A Parent's Perspective	114
A Sibling's Thoughts	120
What Parents and Kids Both Want from Tennis	123

Point 6—Mentorship
Mentors Who Influenced both Jeremy and Tim	128
Modeling Life Fundamentals through Coaching	139
What Kind of Mentor Are You?	143

Point 7—Off-Court Professionalism
Accessing the Best Continuing Education	149
Partnering with Peers: Sharing Best Practices	152
Solutions for Teaching Pro Challenges	155

Match Point
The End Game	160
Final Thoughts	162

Acknowledgments

We are eternally grateful to our family, friends and coaching colleagues who supported us and helped us turn this book idea into a reality.

First and foremost we want to thank our parents for introducing us to the game of tennis in a way that allowed us to love the game and learn the life lessons it has taught us. Specifically we want to thank Dr. William Carl (Jeremy's dad), renowned pastor, international public speaker and a published author of eight books himself, for editing our book and contributing to the book in a way that lays out for our readers a clear understanding of our coaching philosophy.

We offer appreciation to Tim's wife, Helen, for doing the visual designs on the front and back cover. We also want to recognize the other contributors to the book including Feisal Hassan, David Redding, Tim's Mom, Linda Paul, Tim's sister, Sancha Legg, Paul Fisher, and tennis student and friend, Michael Bambha. In addition, we thank Tim's uncle, John Hawker, his father, Peter Bainton, Jeremy's wife, Melissa, and his Mom, Jane Carl, for reading the manuscript for final editing. All of these people provided us the confidence to pursue the dream of writing this book.

We want to thank Peggy Edwards at the Professional Tennis Registry (PTR) who encouraged us along the way and Sandy Davis for taking our picture and making us look better than we actually look in real life!

We also want to thank our fellow pros in the Alexandria, VA area—Leon Cerdena, Brian Clay, Patrick Escalambre, Steve Fiske, Scott Hinkle, Dan Myers, Mike Smith, and Kelly Sykes for their support through this process.

In addition, we appreciate Dimitris Kollaros, Gretchen Thompson, Kathleen O'Brien, and Celeste Jones both for supporting us in writing this book and in our professional development endeavors in general.

We are grateful to the USPTA for supporting our article ideas and the USTA Player Development Staff including Jessica Battaglia, Paul Lubbers and David Ramos for helping us grow as coaches through the USTA High Performance Program. Tim thanks Andrew McPhee, Keely O'Brien, Nestor Bernabe, Cameron Moore, Jim Harp, Brian Parkkonen, Erik Martinez, Bruce Hawtin, Bill Riddle, George Christoforatos, Jim Scott, Alice Hume, Matt Krawczyk, Jason Wnuk, Daniele Albergottie, and many more who have influenced his life and work. Both Jeremy and Tim thank our tennis friend and one of our biggest supporters, David Jackson, and the USTA Mid-Atlantic Section Staff for all their support and encouragement.

Finally, we offer a special thanks to Paula Baird, originally from South Africa and a former Division I player at the University of Alabama Birmingham who has also taught and coached tennis, for her thorough reading of the manuscript and her many helpful suggestions.

Warming Up

Introduction

"What makes a good coach? Complete dedication."
George Halas

Why a new book on tennis coaching written by a guy from Surrey, England and another one from Dallas, Texas? Here's why. We were talking one day about all the great coaches we have known and about our own experiences from coaching and thought it would be a good idea to share some of our conclusions with others.

At first we were talking about these ideas in presentations around the country and were publishing them in various journals and newsletters. The ideas became words. Then keywords became sentences and paragraphs. One thing led to another and voilà this book was born! The product of the UK and the Lone Star State written in the Nation's Capital. Now there's a combination! We are thankful to colleagues around the country who have encouraged us to share our thoughts with a wider audience.

You will see that the book is organized initially with chapter titles as Tennis scores. We do that for a reason. As coaches we are always keeping score and monitoring how we are improving and how we are helping our players improve. You will notice many practical and accessible lists of ideas here. Use the ones that help you the most. But this is more than a book of lists. It's a book that will help you be the best you can be not only as a coach and mentor but also as an ambassador for the game we all love so much.

Now a warning. If you are not interested in either excellence or success then stop reading now because this book is about both. But if you do want to excel and succeed and want your players to do both then keep reading. Before we begin, we want to share a brief word about success that forms the foundation for all our thoughts presented in this book.

What defines success for a coach? Is it the development of top-performing players? Is it putting a smile on someone's face? Or is it about giving people a means of social interaction through playing a sport?

There is no definite answer; it could be one, any, or none of these. That's the thing about success—it is only measured subjectively. The old saying, "One man's trash is another man's treasure" could not be more applicable when discussing what success means to a person. Differences in the meaning of success are created by differences in coaching ideology, an aspect that goes beyond just teaching style.

An industry like tennis coaching has many different options, which is part of the reason that measuring success is difficult, even for the coaches themselves. It's impossible to be successful if you don't know what success is, so the first step to becoming successful is to define what success means for you. Whatever the goal, just make sure it's realistic, or you will find yourself setting the bar too high thus setting yourself up for failure.

So how do you go about measuring success? It's very likely you don't even know what success means for you, and that's perfectly fine. Many successful people started out not even having a clue as to what they wanted from life. In fact, Walt Disney started out writing for a newspaper, and, ironically, was fired for not having good ideas. Or what about Sloane Stephens who, right after winning the 2017 US Open, recounted the story of a coach once telling her she would only ever play Division II college tennis?

Realizing what kind of person you are is the best way to understand how to define success for yourself and the best way to make a difference. Are you a person who needs to see results? Would you be content with coaching a kid who has fun, but doesn't get any better at tennis? Asking self-directed questions such as these provides the first step toward defining success. If coaching people who don't improve isn't fulfilling, then maybe you will need a more competitive atmosphere in which to coach.

The best advice that we can give for realizing success is to "start small, dream big." Success cannot always be defined by the end goal. Be introspective about your accomplishments, and think about what you have already done to make an impact on others' lives. Through time and effort, you will come to see your mark on the world, even if the original goal doesn't work out. In short, the definition of success varies from person to person. In order to become successful, people need to know what success means for them, and what their vision for the future is.

In this book we explore different avenues to success for you as a coach and for your players. Now, we hope you will learn from what we have learned in a way that will help you enjoy teaching and coaching Tennis more than you ever have before!

Jeremy's Journey

It was September 11, 2001. It seemed like a normal day in Washington, D.C., and yet we know there was nothing normal about it. As long as I live I will never forget that day just as my parents will never forget the day JFK was shot and my grandparents will never forget the day Pearl Harbor was attacked. I was a young Capitol Hill staffer working for U.S. Senator Kay Bailey Hutchison of Texas, my home state at the time. I had graduated from Presbyterian College in Clinton, S.C. in 2000 and was just getting my professional work life started in Washington, D.C. I was staying in my college roommate's apartment, sleeping on an air mattress. He had moved to DC a year earlier. I lived in the Alexandria, VA area near Old Town Alexandria, about a 30 minute drive on a good traffic day, to the Russell Senate Office Building on Capitol Hill.

      That particular morning I got a late start and had no idea I would pass right by the Pentagon not long before a plane crashed into it. I remember having the radio on and hearing something about a plane hitting a building in New York City. I thought how awful that was but did not understand how world changing an event it was until I got to work. When I arrived I noticed everyone glued to the TVs in the Senate office with the News blaring the story as a commercial plane flew right into one of the World Trade Centers. Then a couple of minutes later the same thing happened to other World Trade Center, then the Pentagon with the Shanksville, PA crash to follow, the plane that had been headed for the Capitol Building. The Hill was given the evacuate order. So Senator Hutchison quickly and calmly gathered all the staff and let us know we had two choices—we could either try to get home with certain roads blocked off or go to her house on Capitol Hill. Since I knew I'd never make it past the Pentagon which had just been hit, I decided to go with the Senator and other staff who made the same decision. As soon as we arrived at her house we watched in complete horror as the two World Trade Centers collapsed.

I will never forget this next part for the rest of my life. Once in the Senator's house, she immediately got on her computer for all of us to email our loved ones about our safety because all the cell phone connections were blocked. My dad remembers his and my mom's panic trying unsuccessfully to reach me. The Senator sat right next to me, not as my boss, but as a shepherd protecting her flock. She made sure that I typed in my parents' email address and sent the message "I am okay" to them, and did the same with the rest of the staff. My parents lived in Texas at the time. Out of all the things she did as Senator, I know the care she showed for me and her staffers' safety that day was the single greatest and most appreciated action she ever did as a Senator. In a way this message can be translated into coaching because coaching is not about teaching the perfect forehand stroke but about guiding players in purposeful problem solving so they know (while nothing can compare to the horror of 9/11) everything "will be okay" even during the most stressful times of their matches.

Even though working in politics both for a United States Senator and the President of United States at the White House provided incredible experiences, I decided in the summer of 2008 to take the plunge full time in the tennis teaching world. While working in 2007 as Associate Director of External Affairs in the Public and Congressional Affairs Office of the National Credit Union Administration in Alexandria, VA, I began volunteering on weekends coaching some tennis classes at Regency Sport and Health in McLean, VA. I knew pretty quickly that tennis coaching was something I always felt I might be called to pursue. I emailed USPTA Master Professional Feisal Hassan, Tennis Director of Regency Sport and Health in McLean, VA at the time. He gave me a call and we spoke about my interest in exploring tennis teaching as a profession, and just getting a feel for it. After I had volunteered initially by assisting with classes, he let me know of a full time opening that could start in the summer of 2008. I decided to take it and leave government service for good. My initial experience working for Feisal was an incredible introduction to the important principles of coaching, which I will comment on later in this book.

But let me go back to the beginning. Tennis has been my lifelong passion, introduced and inspired by my parents. I was born August 19, 1977 in Richmond, Virginia. My first experience with tennis was when I was 18 months old and my parents hung a Nerf ball on a string in an archway of our house. I would just whack away at that ball with a racquetball racquet for hours at a time. It was fun!

In retrospect I realize my parents never pushed me into tennis; instead they simply presented the game to me and let me enjoy it. I remember going to Wimbledon when I was 11 years old. One day we were at Centre Court watching Boris Becker who was about to become the 1989 Wimbledon Champion. I turned to my dad and said, "I am going to come back here someday." He said, "Okay." I said, "I mean to play." He said, "That sounds great!" The important thing was the fact that he let me figure out on my own how to strive to compete at a very high level. Now, every day as I play with my daughter Maggie, I apply those same principles.

It is no surprise that my parents would have me involved in tennis since they both enjoyed the sport from their high school years on. My mom actually played on her high school tennis team, and my dad played it recreationally in high school. When they met at the University of Tulsa, Dad noticed immediately how well Mom played and decided to focus on improving his own game as quickly as he could to impress Mom. Now at almost 70 he still plays competitively.

My parents' also instilled a love for the game in my brother, David, who is an accomplished actor on stage, television and film and a stand-up comedian in New York City. While he never pursued a career in tennis he has always had a passion for the game. Anytime we see each other we always enjoy playing tennis. When we moved to Texas I was five years old. In junior high and high school I played regularly in USTA Championship level tournaments throughout the state. I played college tennis at Presbyterian College in Clinton, S.C. and was captain of the team my senior year helping lead my fellow players to victory as South Atlantic Conference Champions.

As mentioned earlier, once I graduated from college in 2000, I moved to Washington, D.C. to get experience working in a government job. After serving on the Legislative Staff on Senator Hutchison and subsequently in the White House, I decided to return to my true passion—Tennis. Following a successful career of coaching in the DC Metropolitan area, I joined my coauthor, Tim Bainton, at Mount Vernon Athletic Club as part of the Blue Chip Academy teaching regionally and nationally ranked, high end juniors. Tim and I have been fortunate to learn from each other and help grow the game through our common coaching experiences. Now I teach at Belle Haven Country Club in Alexandria, VA.

My family has always been passionate about education and teaching. My mom, a math and political science major at the University of Tulsa, grew up with a love for education since her mother was a school teacher in Maryville, TN and her dad a school principal. My dad has served as Senior Pastor at First Presbyterian Church in Dallas, TX, President and Professor at Pittsburgh Theological Seminary and currently serves as Senior Pastor of Independent Presbyterian Church in Birmingham, AL. Dad always says a good sermon, "must teach the mind, touch the heart and move the will." A good tennis lesson does the same—teach a skill, inspire a joy and move the player to turn focused practice into skilled match play.

Finally, I have a very supportive wife named Melissa who, though not a tennis player herself, continues to be supportive of my decision to change from government work to teaching tennis full time. She has been a big encourager in all the coaching endeavors I have pursued. Her parents also have a background in education since her mom is a former school principal and her dad a high school biology teacher and counselor.

Jeremy on his Co-author

As a friend and colleague, Tim is the embodiment of respect, support and encouragement. I am grateful for his unselfish desire to help me grow professionally in all aspects of my coaching. His drive to pass along his knowledge to others and learn from others makes it a pleasure to work with him and call him a partner. His passion to improve people's lives on and off the court through tennis is always evident in his daily actions. His commitment and hunger for excellence in the tennis industry and as a person have made him a leader in tennis, coaching, business and mentoring. It is my privilege to co-author this book on coaching with him.

Tim's Tale

The year was 1994 and stars filled the night sky as I watched my hero Stefan Edberg play live for the very first time. The match was held over for bad light but for an eleven-year-old who had fallen in love with tennis, it was magic. I can visualize it like it was yesterday - the beauty of Centre Court, the quiet followed by the roars of the crowd and the beauty of Edberg's game. Another profound moment in my tennis life was in 1999, the final day of the USA vs. GBR Davis Cup tie in Birmingham, England. I attended the event with a group of fellow Surrey teammates organized by my coach. Although we were mildly upset that Great Britain lost the tie, I can still remember the excitement and happiness that filled the air. I can also remember going across the street to a neighbor's house, the only place with cable, to watch the French Open final with my dad the year Muster won.

I was born January 6th, 1983 in Carshalton, and spent all my life in the traditional English village of Chobham Surrey. As a 10-year-old, I was told I wasn't allowed to play on the Village Men's tennis team because "I kept beating all of the players." I later played at Queens Club where I would attend practices and leave school early to attend tournaments.

Playing County Cup for the formidable Surrey with many ATP players as teammates, becoming the 16 and under state champion as a 14-year-old, playing nationals, ITF, internationally: tennis was my identity and I became a part of my generation's rising junior tennis star fabric in the United Kingdom.

I played all sports and loved every minute of it, but it was a profound summer back in 1993 that changed my life forever. I attended a tennis camp at the Chris Lane Tennis Club in Woking, Surrey, and there I met the first coach who would forever shape my love and appreciation for tennis and the art of coaching. Her name was Claire Pollard. I have never been so excited to wake up and do anything in my life because of Claire, a truly magnetizing coach that has gone on to do great things.

Next, I worked with the up and coming legend Justin Sherring, a guy who taught me how to be determined, disciplined and selfless. He would work with me three mornings a week at 6:30 AM for free and then take me to school. He believed in me and looking back I will never be able to express my lifelong appreciation for what he did. Justin was just getting into teaching and determined to be a coach for the same reasons I became one: because he wanted to! He had a larger-than-life personality despite being 5'6 on a good day. However, he would take me to tournaments, support me, root for me and be there for me. He has gone on to make his mark in the game of tennis and I really appreciate all he did for me.

My tennis abilities took me to every part of the country and beyond, competing every weekend on the Adidas Junior circuit that was for the top 16 players in the country. It was quite an experience to leave school on a Friday, do my homework on a train to random places such as Darlington, Sunderland and Wrexham to arrive at midnight to some affordable hotel, play four matches in two days, return and then attend school again Monday morning. These times were the best of times.

I attended St. George's College in Weybridge on a tennis scholarship, and my game truly thrived there. The school had so many assets for tennis players to utilize, and all types of courts: clay, grass, and hard as well as both indoor and outdoor courts. The school was a hotbed for young talent and a warm-up venue for Wimbledon where I had seen many top players develop. I established a strong bond with the faculty at the school. I dearly loved Mr. Peak, the headmaster, and a man of incredible integrity, Mr. Witter, an American with more wit than you could imagine who taught English, Ms. Frawley an Oxbridge-educated tutor who taught me the value of attendance, discipline and respect. Mr. Watters, a genius of a teacher who taught my 'A' level politics and philosophy classes, taught me how to think, to be challenged and to improve constantly in everything I did. I truly loved those days and through great teaching, without knowing it, they provided me a backbone for great coaching.

Now to answer the "Why did you come to America?" question. I arrived in Fairfax VA, to attend the mighty George Mason University seven days before 9/11. In reflection, being in a foreign land with such a tragedy occurring on your doorstep meant that my illusions of playing one year of college tennis on a gap year and then returning to a deferred place at the London School of Economics were forever gone. This was my home and my family for four years and beyond. The Northern Virginia, DC area has been home and a place to build a business, family, friends, and opportunity ever since.

After school, I went into coaching despite opportunities to move into many other professions; this is where I wanted to be. I started from scratch earning $9 an hour in 2005 to becoming one of the most successful industry leaders in the country a decade later. The key is to be always learning, treat everyone equally and bring as many people into your world as possible. Stay hungry, stay humble and ultimately never stop loving the art of coaching. I hope you enjoy this book as much as Jeremy and I enjoyed writing it.

Tim on his co-author

Jeremy is one of the most gracious, loyal and intelligent friends and colleagues that I know. He defines the professional coach: always on time, always presentable, and always prepared. He is a coach who lives his life by the same standard that he demands of his students. His passion and love for the game and the art of coaching have solidified him as one of the best development coaches in the country and a respected force on improving the industry through continuing education, writing and speaking.

Point 1
First Serve:
Three Foundations of Coaching

15 Love - 15 Reasons to Be a Coach

"Coaching is by far the best profession you could ever be in—
You have the chance to be significant."
Lou Holtz

Through our years in the tennis world, it has become apparent to us that people enter the tennis coaching arena for a variety of reasons. Coaching is more than just a job to pay the bills, or a "stop-gap" between jobs. Actually, serving as a tennis coach is the greatest and most rewarding profession of all. This is the first in a series of reasons we do what we do as coaches and why we enjoy it so much. Here are some other reasons, fifteen to be exact.

Privilege—Teaching is the best way to have a direct and long-term effect on somebody's life. As a tennis coach, the variety of people you get to meet and interact with allows you to develop friendships and relationships, something your typical 9-5 job will not offer.

Health Benefits—In a day and age when people with office jobs are advocating standing desks and other similar alternatives to sitting, health is a primary concern in the workplace. Coaching gives you the luxury of being in charge of your own health and promotes an active lifestyle. Active people are healthier people; several studies have shown how exercise reduces stress as well as one's risk for heart disease. As coaches, we have always appreciated the active aspect of our jobs, and we are reminded of it every time we step on the court.

Network—We have spoken about this subject in our Partnerships presentations and Tennis Entrepreneurship, but being a coach gives you access to a diverse and valuable network of clients and businesses, more so than any other profession. We have often made the point that if tennis coaches know the value of their Rolodex (now gathered digitally), tennis would be the most powerful sport in the country through expansion and diversification. It is without question that every person with whom we do business directly or indirectly works with us because of references we have gained from being on the court or in the industry. The potential is limitless.

Demographics—From whom you coach to where you go, being a coach allows you to connect with people of all different races, religions and backgrounds. The ability to be immersed in this diversity of culture is very meaningful to us since we are able to connect and learn from people in all walks of life.

Opportunity—Sports are a major key to success for many people, and as coaches, we have the privilege of being able to watch our students unlock their full potential. Physically and emotionally, you will be grateful for the roller-coaster ride since coaches develop many relationships along the way. We have been fortunate enough to be invited to the US Open, to walk behind the ropes watching famous golfers at the PGA and invited to see Pacquiao vs. Mayweather fight in Las Vegas. However, we have also had the honor of working with multiple charities, to participate on boards, committees and a variety of other organizations that help others. None of this would have been possible if we weren't coaches, and we have enjoyed all of it every step of the way.

Longevity—Having an incredibly healthy and active lifestyle is a surefire way to enjoy a long and consistent career. We have a dear friend, a successful tennis director who retired at 55, who teaches 15 hours a week for a premium from his beach house based on his name and experience. With endless possibilities, we never lose our love of the sport; so retirement is different from traditional workspaces. However, we can pivot and still make good money part-time while enjoying some of the finer things later in life. Although some will say that injury is a risk in this job, those who take care of their bodies through routine stretching and other injury prevention techniques will remain healthy throughout their lives.

Continuing Education—When Tim graduated college, he mucked around for a bank in New York, but later came back to tennis and realized he had no name or brand. Tim hadn't won a Grand Slam, so he needed to make his name through hard work, but most importantly through a thirst for education. He has spent a lot of time reading books, watching videos, and listening to podcasts that have helped him become a better teacher, coach, and businessman. Additionally, teaching, mentoring and learning from other people have enabled him to become better and better informed. And most of this could be said about Jeremy, too.

Challenges—Figuring out how to beat an opponent makes us stronger if we are able to learn from our mistakes. We have made many mistakes but are not afraid to put ourselves out there, and that is the key; when you make mistakes, own them and embrace them. Challenge yourself to be better tomorrow than you are today on and off the court. As a coach, you can make your own future but also directly affect the future of the clients you serve. That added pressure can be an amazing tool if you embrace it and find solutions to make things work. Whether it is business, coaching, or just life, people who can solve problems will always be the most successful.

Realizing Goals—Coaching allows you to see results being achieved on the court—physically and emotionally for players, and financially and operationally for yourself. In this sport, we set goals for our players, and if you are a great coach you mandate short, middle and long-term goals for your students, and you hold them accountable to achieve those goals while giving them all of the tools they need to succeed. As coaches, our possibilities are limitless as to what we can achieve if we really put our minds to it. The court becomes our canvas to accomplish what we want. We have the ability to do this in our profession and as former athletes, we understand the need for dedication and understand the fruits that discipline will give us.

Travel—Where do we begin? When we first started coaching we were excited to travel to weekend tournaments, but through years of coaching, we have seen all of the opportunities that this job offers in terms of travel. We have close friends who spend multiple weeks and weekends speaking at conferences and tournaments all around the world. These travels go far beyond the United States, including one traveling pro gig in Jamaica.

Satisfaction—Everything from seeing toddlers with racquet in hand and a smile on their faces, to having a player play at Kalamazoo or San Diego leads to a sense of accomplishment that is unique to the tennis teaching profession. This job is meaningful to us on a spectrum that would not exist in any other profession. Coaching represents a fishbowl of opportunities to enjoy outcomes that we may or may not have control over, but either way, it makes for an extremely satisfying career not quite knowing what will make us smile next.

Flexibility—Despite many long hours and strange structures to our days, if we are organized we can actually beat the rat race and be fortunate to have certain hours and days free to do things we need and/or want to do. Our hours are not conventional, but the best coaches learn to use their time efficiently. A coach's day is not always 9-5; it can be as extreme as Noon to 1:00, 3:00 to 5:00, and 6:00 to 10:00 pm, which means we might have more time earlier in the day.

Financial Freedom—Simple! WORK MORE, EARN MORE; in other words, be creative in growing your programs and you will earn more. Tennis coaches and pros are not limited by an annualized increase like government employees. It's an economic system that creates more challenges but also more opportunities to make money. We both live by this motto: "Take care of the client and the rest takes care of itself." We work in a profession where early on the more we grind the more we make, but the more we can develop a footprint for who we are as coaches, the more successful we can become. Take that seed and do what you want with it. You want to own a club? Do it! We are not constrained by the same restrictions that make people successful doctors or lawyers. Being coaches allows us the freedom and foundation to carve our own paths to success.

Prestige—Tim remembers before he met his wife, he was on a date with a girl who worked on Capitol Hill, and it was a black-tie event. Here is his version of what happened: "We sat at a table of twelve and made small talk with others. Someone asked me, 'What do you do?' I told him I was a tennis coach, and he responded with a smirk and asked, 'What do you really do?' It was then that I realized that I was above the normal posturing and rat race; I was a coach, which meant I owned my own business, worked my own hours, continually found resources to educate myself and didn't care who judged me. I have been going to school since I was 4 when I first hit a tennis ball. In other words, I am proud of being a coach. Jeremy is too." Coaching is an amazing, liberating and humbling profession that will enable you to meet remarkable people and call them friends, travel the country and the world, and make everyone else you know outside of this profession envious as hell that you are a coach.

Individuality and Teamwork—Tennis has taught us both that, although the game is usually focused on the individual, one of the things that makes tennis coaching unique is that it requires teamwork. As a coach, you are your own individual and have your own team, but that extends beyond the client and into the professional development world. You are in charge of what you want to do and where you want to go. You are able to take people with you and learn from everyone. Everyone is a potential client and business partner. Build your own self-image, your own team, and your own brand to be successful. Focus on yourself as much as you do the client; it only increases the value that you bring to the client and will lead to increased business, obtainable and maintainable price points, and individual and financial success.

30 Love - 30 Skills Every Coach Needs

"Most people get excited about games, but I've got to be excited about practice, because that's my classroom."
Pat Summitt

"Spectacular performances are preceded by spectacular preparation."
Frank Giampaolo

The list below is something for all of us to aspire to; many of the skills some of us already have naturally while others need to develop them. Few coaches have all of these qualities when they start their career, but we have witnessed many great coaches who have them. We have continued to add and adapt in order to create the comprehensive list below.

Patience - Learning new skills takes time, something every coach needs to be aware of. Some students learn quickly, while others may take longer; however, it is the coach's job never to lose sight of the goals no matter how long it takes players to reach them.

Desire - Effective coaches actually *want* to teach others. Good coaches embrace the idea of bringing about change by helping and teaching, strong values that make a coach so much more than just a teacher.

Approachable – Good coaches are not intimidating; they are flexible and relatable so that students feel they are in a comfortable environment where they can ask questions and learn without being held back by a fear of making mistakes.

Professionalism – As in any job, coaching requires professionalism. It would be difficult for students to take their coaches seriously if they showed up to work late or if they were dressed inappropriately for coaching. If the coach is serious about teaching, the student will be serious about learning.

Likeability – A coach must have a personality that mixes well with the students they are coaching. Coaching is all about communication, and there is no bigger deterrent to learning than someone who does not like, thus probably does not trust, his or her coach.

Humor – Of course being funny is a quality that many people admire, but in the coaching world, humor serves more of a purpose than just providing entertainment. It creates a more relaxing environment and reduces the stress of making mistakes.

Compassion – Coaches really do care about what they do. They do not pick this profession just to pay the bills, but because they want to make a difference. Students recognize these kinds of coaches and will feel more inspired to learn if it shows.

Industry Presence – Building a name and a brand is just as important for a coach as it is for a journalist or a businessperson. Successful coaches have created a name for themselves through hard work and dedication, which allows them to expand their horizons and further their careers.

Self-Awareness – Coaches understand how their body language and words affect players. Good coaches do not discourage players because they present themselves in an appropriate manner for teaching that allows players to thrive.

Preparedness – A coach will always have multiple tricks up his or her sleeve in anticipation of one particular teaching technique that might not be effective. Creating a plan beforehand is always crucial. And yet, as in American football, one always needs to be prepared to call 'an audible.'

Great Listening Skills – Effective coaching is a team effort and requires the coach and the student to both be on the same page. Coaches cannot give advice if they do not understand what is holding a student back from learning, and so the best coaches always listen then tweak their teaching style to the needs of their students.

Ability to Give Constructive Criticism – Coaches must recognize that their ability to communicate effectively lies in both their body language and through what they say. A good coach will keep a positive attitude in order not to discourage a player from learning, and gives advice in a way that makes sense to the student.

Can Also Receive Criticism Graciously – Coaching is a two-way street, and the best coaches appreciate suggestions about how they can improve themselves. Good coaches are able to use this information to improve particular aspects of their craft, thus becoming even more effective.

Ability to Understand One's Own Limitations – A coach always puts the player first, and if that means that there are certain skills that are beyond the coach's expanse of knowledge, then it is his or her responsibility to recognize that and either figure out a way to help the player or find another teaching pro who can.

Goal Setting – Goals are vital to growth in the sports world, and a coach must know how to set goals that motivate the student to work hard, but that also remain realistic. Typically coaches will set short term, medium term, and long-term goals so that the student can feel a sense of progression when these goals are realized.

Something Extra – Coaches are typically good listeners, and that is a quality that makes them easy to talk to, which creates an air of comfort. As mentors, coaches should be able to give advice that goes above and beyond simply teaching skills, but rather things that can be applied to life in general.

Problem Solver – Problems sometimes arise when teaching or coaching any sport, whether students don't understand what is being taught, miscommunication either way, or a variety of other things that can go wrong. Fortunately, this is something that coaches are used to dealing with, which is what makes them very good at finding alternative solutions.

Idea Sharing – Oftentimes, figuring out how to solve problems requires more than just critical thinking. Coaches collaborate with each other to bounce ideas around about how to teach certain skills more effectively or to brainstorm creative ways to overcome challenges.

Optimistic but Realistic - Nobody will become the next Roger Federer in a year, of course, but coaches do set goals for their students that they feel are attainable. Optimism is motivation, and keeping students motivated is the best way for them to learn.

Accountability – While it is very easy to put the blame on someone else, the best coaches instead take responsibility for any failures or mistakes. If a player is having difficulty with the same stroke for months, even though the coach has tried several different teaching methods, the coach realizes that blaming the player for his or her failure to learn will only contaminate the learning atmosphere. Instead the coach will take it as his or her duty to communicate effectively.

Willingness to evolve – The sports world is constantly changing, and coaches must adapt to these changes in order to stay in the game. Whether it is through learning new changes in the game or new teaching ideas, it is important that a coach stay dedicated to becoming the best he or she can be.

Constantly Learning – In order to be the best teacher, a coach must have an extensive knowledge of what to teach and how to teach it, and the only way to do this is through learning.

Encouraging – There will be setbacks in any sport that can lead players to feel discouraged, but in tennis, this is exceptionally prevalent because of its nature as an individual sport. It is the duty of the coach to provide not only the physical teaching support that players need but also emotional support in the form of encouragement to keep players on track and motivated.

Leadership – A coach leads by example, and one characteristic of a good leader is the ability to persist through any sort of adversity. This trait goes beyond patience; a leader must show strength and determination; it's what makes good coaches good leaders.

Mentor – Coaches are not just there to teach skills. They work with their students to help them solve problems through teamwork and collaboration, which are skills that can be applied far outside the realm of sports.

Consistency – Coaches keep a similar teaching style and tweak it depending on their students, but do not make erratic changes. Consistency provides clarity for the goals of both the player and the coach.

Objectivity – Although it is important for coaches to have a high emotional IQ, sometimes it can be beneficial to be fact-of-the-matter in certain situations. Coaches will often try to be objective when it comes to a player making mistakes in order to show them what is going wrong without clouding facts with feelings. For example, if a player misses several shots in a row and calls him/herself bad at tennis, a coach might respond by saying the player simply hit the ball too hard.

Emotional Intelligence – This is a trait that is extremely important, especially in an individual sport like tennis. Many say that a tennis match is played on two fronts: on the court and in the mind. It is a coach's job to understanding feelings such as disappointment and frustration and turn them into something positive for the players they are coaching.

Creative – Good coaches will not do the same drill over and over again if they notice it's not an effective means of teaching. The best coaches often think outside the box in order to find a method that works for a particular player.

Humble – Humility is essential to good coaching because it gives the coach the perspective of the student, whereas coaches who gloat only make players feel discouraged and overwhelmed. Understanding a player's thoughts and feelings helps coaches to communicate more effectively.

Ultimately, coaching is a privilege and a chance to utilize a variety of skills, some that are part of our natural DNA and others that we need to learn or seek out better solutions to approaching problems.

40 Love - 40 Goals Coaches Should Try to Attain

"A good coach can change a GAME.
A great coach can change a LIFE."
John Wooden

Every professional should set goals and a means to attain them, and tennis coaches are no different. In fact, coaches are typically very goal driven people, and whether it is advancing their professional career or attaining a personal goal, setting goals will foster self-improvement, create a healthier lifestyle, and promote intellectual growth. Goal setting can be broken down into several categories, including personal, professional, physical, intellectual, and financial goals. Every coach should set goals, but here are forty, in particular that should stand out as a guideline:

Personal Goals —

Work-Life Balance - Balancing personal life and working life is a challenge that every person faces, especially coaches. Tennis coaches work odd hours, sometimes as extreme as 9 AM to 9 PM. So it is of particular importance that coaches learn how to juggle personal and professional time remembering that making enough money to cover costs and reach financial goals can only be achieved when personal equilibrium is also reached.

Finding Mentors - Mentors are more than just teachers or friends; they are a source of inspiration to encourage others to find their own path in life and help promote specific career options. Having somebody who has gone through similar experiences is vitally important for success since the advice good mentors offer is invaluable. For coaches who are interested in starting their own business, a task that requires immense amounts of effort and time, mentors provide a stable base of support.

Finding Passion - There is a wide array of options available to coaches. Whether it is serving as a teaching pro at a club, assisting community tennis programs, or coaching on the pro tour, it is important that coaches discover how they want to continue their passion for teaching professionally while at the same time growing in knowledge.

Maintaining High Levels of Motivation - Coaching is a very rewarding and humbling profession; however, it is by no means easy, and burnout can come quickly if one isn't careful. To remain highly motivated, coaches need to remember the joy they felt when they taught their first lesson or clinic. In addition, stress management skills are essential to coaching since it requires sustained interaction with all kinds of people all day long.

Being Proactive and not Reactive - Although this is a good life philosophy in general, it is one that coaches should constantly remember. To avoid becoming overwhelmed by work, coaches should always plan ahead. For example, if coaches do not properly plan lessons ahead of time, they may find themselves working a long shift, then planning lessons for another one or two hours on top of the work that's already ahead of them. Proactive coaches keep organized schedules to keep track of events and are always on-task setting examples for others.

Cultivating Long-lasting Relationships - In a profession based on collaboration with others, coaches make new friends and develop relationships quickly. However, it is important to ensure that the friendships and relationships that are helpful continue. Between work and personal life, it can be a comfort to have friends to confide in both for stress reduction and meaningful personal interaction.

Chameleon Coaching - Knowing who your players are and how to present new strokes or strategies to them is an essential component of successful coaching. For example, coaches would not teach five-year-olds the same way they would teach adults. Every person learns differently, and it is a coach's job to recognize and adapt.

Becoming Great Listeners – Effective coaching means that both coach and player must be on the same page, which requires active listening and communication. Players may notice something specific about their game that they would like to improve or may even give the coach feedback about whether certain aspects of their teaching style are working or not. It's imperative that coaches listen carefully to the suggestions players make since their readiness for learning will be higher if they are able to articulate an area of weakness themselves.

Professional Goals —
Becoming Certified - One of the first steps in a professional tennis coaching career is to receive the necessary certifications for teaching. However obvious this may seem, certifications make an enormous difference in creating a more professional atmosphere as well as making coaches more reputable and authoritative.

Creating a Network and Establishing Clientele - Another important professional step for tennis coaches is to create a strong network, including other coaches, and mentors, who can bridge the gap between amateur and professional. Additionally, having a basis for a reliable audience of clients is important for both revenue and reputation.

Auditing Industry Presence - The most successful coaches have always known what their place is in the market and how they influence others. They never overestimate their value while constantly working to increase their standing among their own peers.

Establishing a Brand - In order to become successful, coaches must make a name for themselves in the industry. Creating a network and a reputation are part of this, but coaches also must put their unique personality and philosophy out there to make the brand fresh and new. Remember the approach to teaching and coaching that has brought you great success creating your brand, and don't try to be something you're not.

Becoming a Mentor - Mentoring is one of the most rewarding aspects of coaching because it is an awesome responsibility, one that allows coaches to have an impact on players' lives long term. By giving advice, providing encouragement and support, while at the same time modeling best practices, coaches help shape more than players' games. They turn players into life-long learners who never stop improving and being the best they can.

Exploring Industry Options - Coaching itself is a very flexible profession, but there are limitless choices in regards to teaching tennis, whether it is through traveling abroad, working at a facility, or assisting with special needs coaching. It is possible that coaches may not recognize better options that exist in the industry, which is why coaches should always be open to new ideas and options.

Publishing Articles and Speaking at Conferences - This is a goal that all coaches should consider since it's the best way for them to create a name for themselves in the tennis world. Records of coaches speaking or written articles can be found by anybody anywhere on the Internet, and it is not only a great way for coaches to boost their reputation, but also to give back by sharing their ideas and experiences.

Owning a Business - Starting a business is a difficult task and takes time, money, and energy, but it is rewarding and is worth every second of effort put into it. Owning a business allows coaches to set their own hours, create a vision and shape a culture as they develop a reputation for success.

Intellectual Goals —
Becoming Valuable Sources of Information - Every coach should want to be the go-to person when anybody asks anything related to tennis. The best teachers are the best learners, and for coaches, learning is vital to keeping up with the dynamic changes in the realm of tennis.

Continuing Education: Learning is a major part of any profession since more education means more credibility and thus more business. In tennis especially, because it is such a fast-changing industry, coaches will come to realize that they may need more education to remain competitive.

Education Transcending Tennis Industry - Successful coaches have realized that they need a wide expanse of knowledge that surpasses solely tennis. What if a coach wanted to start his or her own business? The information needed to accomplish this comes from many sources, including successful people completely unrelated to tennis.

"Ferocious" reading - Reading is still one of the easiest ways to expand vocabulary, general knowledge, generate ideas, and delve into imagination. Productive reading is a great benefit to coaches that are motivated to continue learning throughout their career and professional life.

Continued Self-reflection - Taking a more intellectual approach to coaching can be one of the best ways to improve. Analyzing which teaching methods seem to be best understood, which lessons yield the best results, and other self-directed questions are aspects of coaching that should be taken seriously.

Accessing a Diverse Group Outside of Work Life - In order to generate new ideas and foster intellectual growth, a diverse group of people, one with people of varying age, race, religion, and ideology, is recommended. A group of similar-minded people would just agree on nearly every topic, so no new perspectives could be shared. When people from different backgrounds come together with opposing philosophies, many new points of view have a chance to surface.

Developing Problem Solving Skills - Problems arise for a tennis coach in all sorts of situations, whether it is figuring out how to teach a certain topic or dealing with parents. Through experience, coaches can become adept mediators and problems solvers. First, coaches listen carefully to make sure they understand the dimensions of a certain problem, then use all available means of information at their disposal to solve those problems reasonably and fairly.

Studying a Foreign Language - Bilingualism is increasingly important in today's society. Learning a second language requires commitment and effort. However, certain languages such as Spanish and French are prevalent in the workplace; in addition, the ability to communicate through other languages allows for greater opportunities for travel and employment.

Physical —
Maintaining a High Level of Tennis Proficiency - It is still important for coaches to perform at a competitive level so they can assess and deal with the challenges that high-level players face directly. It becomes much easier for coaches to explain and work around problems that they have dealt with personally.

Incorporating Injury Prevention Methods – It's obvious that injuries are painful and hinder work ability and many other inconveniences. Coaches should always make it a goal and a habit to stretch with a purpose for 15-20 minutes before exercise. Practicing Yoga and getting massages are also great ways to help loosen muscles to increase flexibility thus avoid injury.

Practicing Healthy Nutrition - Coaches who are going to be on the court for eight hours need to make sure they are aware of what they consume, and that they are getting enough calories and protein to sustain an active lifestyle. Breakfast is absolutely vital to provide energy for the remainder of the day and should be consumed every day.

Awareness of Sleep Schedule - Coaches need plenty of rest and a healthy sleep schedule to maintain their active lifestyles. So part of work and life balance means coaches need to make sure that their personal life after work does not interfere with the sleep that they need.

Athletic Hobbies - Coaches should try to find another athletic interest other than tennis for recreation or even for cross-training. Playing sports as a hobby is a great way to reduce stress and stay active while having fun, and certain sports can be used for recreation and to build muscles that aren't used in tennis, such as swimming and cycling.

Periodization - Coaching is a sport that can be very physically taxing, and it is essential that coaches know how much strain they can handle before they risk injury. In some scenarios, a coach may want to take a day or a few days off to rest his or her body to prevent injury.

Developing a Sustainable Lifestyle – When coaches are on the court for eight or more hours a day, physical strain can compound quickly, increasing risk of injury. Coaches need to think what it will take to maintain this activity level for ten, twenty, or even more years.

Drinking Water and Replenishing Electrolytes - Drinking water is vitally important to health, especially since coaches are such active people. Water helps aid recovery and prevent dehydration, which can cause muscle cramps. Additionally, many necessary electrolytes are lost through sweat, so whether it is an electrolyte drink or a salty snack, electrolytes help to minimize injuries and prevent cramping.

Financial —
Learning Budgeting Skills - Any professional needs to know how to create and follow a budget; it's a life skill that everybody needs. A well-rounded budget should contain expenses, savings and investments, spending money, and charity money. It should be organized and created with a purpose, as it is a guideline for all of a professional's finances. Some coaches employ financial advisors to assure a good long-term plan for their economic future.

Creating a Plan for Retirement - Similar to a budget, creating a retirement fund is a goal that every professional should work toward immediately after obtaining a steady source of income. In the long run, having a steady source of income after retirement will make life much easier since most coaches do not continue working after age sixty-five.

Owning Property – The idea of purchasing real-estate represents a huge financial goal, one that requires careful planning, saving and investing. Whether it is personal property or land and buildings that eventually become a tennis club, coaches need sound advice before making such a large investment.

Understanding Legalese - Anybody who is starting a business will need to understand the laws, legal terminology, and other legalities that are associated with such an ambitious endeavor. It is well worth the time and money to hire an attorney who is schooled and experienced in startup business law.

Diversifying Investments - Diversification is a basic idea that is used by every wise investor. It's the principle of not putting all of your eggs in one basket; there are multiple contingencies in place in case one investment fails. A well-rounded financial portfolio yields much better results than one that is heavily weighted towards a particular investment.

Seeking Sponsorships - Sponsorships do not always need to be a partnership with large companies; in fact, there are several ways to be sponsored or create partnerships. Public speaking is a great example of this, where some companies may even pay a coach to give a presentation. Opportunities exist everywhere if you are willing to look in the right places.

Creating a Charity Fund - Giving back to the community is great way to contribute to the well-being of society, whether through donations or through free programs. It could be just as basic as donating to a nonprofit or even as big as creating a program for low-income children to learn tennis. Whatever the case, giving to charity demonstrates a strength of moral character.

Understanding Tax Law - Every person who has a budget should be able to recognize how much he or she owes in taxes, and budget accordingly. To have a big expense just show up out of the blue could be devastating, so it is important to take the time to study the taxation laws in the municipality in which you are coaching.

Through self-development and goal setting, professionals can accomplish whatever they set their minds to as long as they develop a particular method for doing so and are willing to put in the effort required. Goal setting represents an amazing way to attain achievements creating a rhythmic cycle of success where the professional is incentivized to accomplish more, finally yielding a real sense of satisfaction after completion.

Point 2
Coaching Fundamentals

5 Building Blocks

"A mentor is someone who allows you to see the hope inside yourself."
Oprah Winfrey

Tennis is one of the hardest sports to play and coach. However, it can be the most rewarding if we use five foundational blocks: **Committed, Organized, Attentive, Creative, and Heartfelt (COACH).**

1. Committed – Being a tennis coach takes complete commitment, especially when we can see it as a "calling" more than a career. While any certified coach has to complete requirements for certification and ongoing continuing education, it is important that coaches take steps to show real commitment to their students' growth as well as their own professional growth. Below are some simple and effective ways to accomplish this:
Watch your students play in tournaments. When you recognize improvement in their match play, let them know it as a way of reinforcing what you've taught them in lessons. In addition, use software like Dartfish, CMV or other similar real-time video editing programs to create and send videos to students and parents, highlighting places where they clearly show improvement.

2. Organized – An organized coach in practice will translate into an organized player and problem solver in a match. This goes beyond having a lesson plan ready or showing up 10 minutes early to have everything set up. Below are some effective ways to show your organizational skills to students and parents at your club:
After each session has ended, provide evaluation forms for parents on their child's progress recommending what class or drill the student should do next.

Provide new ideas to grow your program and bring new students. For example, to develop more tournament players, hold in-house tournaments to help students get used to the pressure of tournament play. To help young players understand the fun of competition, hold a Games and Tournament Red Ball night with music, pizza, and prizes. After the event, send a thank you email or letter that includes a picture of the group to all the parents.

3. Attentive – When we think of being attentive, we think of the legendary basketball coach John Wooden's quote, "It's the little details that are vital. Little things make big things happen." Below are some examples of how being attentive can go a long way:

Parents like to see that you care about their child as a person first and an athlete second. Most children play other sports and participate in other activities. If you know they had an event such as a dance recital or soccer match, ask them about it. Be attentive to tennis-specific items, such as whether the child is left-handed or what grip the student uses in the ready position for returns of serve.

If parents ask why you corrected something, give them productive and purposeful reasoning for your suggestions and let them know specifically how it will help the child in the long run. This approach will help lead to more commitment from the student and the parent.

4. Creative – A coach's ability to be creative in setting up a fun atmosphere is one of the most important foundations for coaching. Note the following statistic on children dropping out of sports from this CNN article, "How to make your kids hate sports without really trying," by Kelly Wallace on Jan. 21, 2016 (www.cnn.com/2016/01/21/health/kids-youth-sports-parents).
"Seventy percent of children leave organized sports by the age 13, according to research by the National Alliance for Sports. Let's put it this way: If your daughter or son plays on a soccer team, seven out of 10 of the members of that team won't be playing soccer or

any organized sport whatsoever by the time they enter their teenage years."

The same statistic is highlighted in an article titled "Why Kids Quit Sports" published in Coaching, Problems in Youth Sports, Sports Parenting by John O'Sullivan on Tuesday, May 5, 2015 (changingthegameproject.com/why-kids-quit-sports). "As I have stated here many times, 70% of children are dropping out of organized sports by age of 13." The O'Sullivan article goes on to mention the main reasons why kids walk away from sports – it's no longer fun and they are afraid to make mistakes. Below are ways tennis coaches can help students overcome those barriers:

'Serving advice' should be positive and productive so the student can apply those tips when struggling in a match. One way to practice this is to play 12-point tiebreaks with your students. If during the 12-point tiebreak they miss the first serve, have them remember the tips before they hit their second serves so you know that they are thinking about positive and productive ways to handle the situation.

Explain that the serve sets up the forehand and backhand. For example, you could have your students play a 12-point tiebreak, and if they successfully apply a specific serve-plus-one-shot strategy – e.g., serve out wide on the deuce side, which pulls the opponent off the court then hit a forehand drive down the line and if they win the point, tell them they get two points instead of one.

Have serving games early in your practices that allow kids to compete from the beginning. Making a game of serving to a certain part of the box is a fun way for children to learn how to serve. This approach also helps them understand that missing a serve is part of the game of tennis.

The same game approach can be done with the return of serve. You can have two teams and call it "tag team return of serve." Each team has multiple players taking turns one at a time serving and returning. Every time one team completes a successful serve and return, that team gets a point. The first team to seven points wins.

Base all the games you play on problem solving. You can do a game called "wheel of fortune" using an app on an iPad, or create one that has different wheels based on spins, style of play, etc. There are two players. The coach spins and wherever it lands, one player has to play with that style of play against another player who also has to play based on how the wheel is spun for him or her.

5. Heartfelt – It is not until your students realize how much you care about tennis that they will begin to understand how much you know about the sport. Below are heartfelt actions that will keep you motivated and show your true passion for the game as a coach:

Go to tournaments and watch your students, then provide specific feedback after matches.

Spend 10 minutes after a lesson giving parents specific feedback on their child's progress.

Hit with new members at the club when you have downtime and then provide them with names of members as potential hitting partners.

Encourage fellow coaches to go above and beyond to help all the students they teach. Remember that your encouragement as a coach is what fuels a successful program with energy, creativity, and continuity.

We hope these principles will guide you in a sport that can be very challenging at times, but tennis is the most rewarding sport you could ever coach!

Chameleon Coach

"The delicate balance of mentoring someone
is not creating them in your own image,
but giving them the opportunity to create themselves."
Steven Spielberg

In a college classroom (not so) far, far away...the professor's monotonous voice drowned out all other noises; the birds stopped singing, the rustling of the leaves quieted, and the world seemed still. The only other audible sound was a few distinct snores from students, heads slumped on their desks and shoulders rolled over their ears. Boredom may not kill, but it freezes. Moments in time are suspended in a solution of ennui; desire for accomplishment becomes stale, and passion turns into apathy.

Boredom is poison, something that all coaches should avoid. In order to better mold with their players, coaches can pretend that they are a chameleon, a sly, sneaky creature who is adept at blending into any surrounding. Some players respond very well to positive reinforcement, some may require a visual example to understand a particular lesson, and others may just need to have fun in order to learn. Whatever the motive, it is a coach's responsibility to identify and use that incentive to catalyze the player's passion for the sport.

Every player has a different learning style. Although this may seem a cliché, it is actually quite important in understanding how to go about planning lessons that adapt well to the way the player learns best. Both teachers and coaches adapt their lessons and styles to the players that are being coached. For example, an adult may be content hitting for an hour and practicing groundstrokes, but younger kids often do not respond well to repetitive, monotonous tasks. In order to teach thoroughly and purposefully, a coach needs the qualities of a CHAMELEON. And they include the following, which spell out the word "Chameleon":

Character - Displaying good character makes a coach more respectable. If anybody were to ask a kid to describe whether their teachers were "good or bad," they generally would not think in terms of effectiveness or even ability, but rather whether or not they appreciate the teacher's personality. People tend to judge others based on character, and for a profession that can rely heavily on reputation as a means of attracting business, coaches must remain personable.

Helpfulness - Giving advice is easy, but the difficult part is helping players in a way that they can comprehend. There is a fine line between lecture and guidance, and the coach needs to understand where this line lies in order to tailor ideas to that specific person. Simply instructing a player to "hit up" on the ball may not work in all cases, and sometimes in order to be helpful, a coach needs to be creative. For example, if a player is hitting a serve into the net several times in a row, one creative solution could be to have that player kneel on a padded surface and try to get a serve in while kneeling.

Awareness - Being aware of what your player needs to succeed is one of the biggest jobs of a coach. Coaches need to be keen on observing details, since in the sport of tennis, the smallest things can make huge differences. Every player has different flaws that need to be corrected, whether it is as clear as stroke form, or as minute as exact footwork patterns. The ability to identify and creatively fix these flaws is a skill learned through experience with coaching.

Maturity - One of the biggest parts of maturity is the willingness to put in extra work, even if it is not required or entirely necessary. Coaches need to remain organized and have a set schedule that they follow.

Energy - Having high energy motivates players to do their best. If a coach is lethargically bumping a ball back and forth with a player, how is the player supposed to be incentivized to do any better? Players can only learn as much as the coach teaches them, and this should be done through setting an example. Energetic coaches also provide motivation for playing a higher level of tennis since they inspire others through their energy to play harder.

Language - Whether it is verbal or body language, a coach needs to be able to communicate effectively in order to connect with the player. While some players may be perfectly fine with an instructor verbally telling them how to hit a particular shot or how to use footwork effectively, others may not learn from listening. Coaches may sometimes need to think creatively in order to get a message across such as playing games that secretly require players to focus on a certain aspect of their game without knowing. Good communication is a vital component of effective coaching.

Empathetic - Coaches need to recognize that the player is first of all a person, and secondly, a tennis player. Players will often encounter certain difficulties in improving, and coaches should prevent players from getting discouraged. Coaches will need a high level of emotional intelligence in order to understand how players feel and the best way for them to improve.

Optimistic - Every player responds well to positive encouragement, which is especially important both for those starting the sport, and those who want to play competitively. Tennis is played on two fronts: on the court and in the mind. As with other individual sports, there is no team to be blamed for mistakes that a player may make. Tennis players often blame themselves harshly for points that go awry, and this guilt can compound into frustration. An optimistic coach is able to take a player's blame and use it constructively to help the player grow.

Non-judgmental - One of the most amazing aspects of tennis is that it attracts such a wide variety of individuals, and people are able to play the sport competitively and casually.

Coaches should never judge others based on their athletic ability or anything else so they can create an environment where players feel comfortable to learn and play tennis.

     Every player has his/her own unique way of learning, and coaches need to identify this style and adapt. Effective coaches bring character, creativity, and positive attitude to the table, rather than just showing off that they are experienced tennis players. Through these characteristics, coaches can become a source of inspiration and mentorship for others.

Creating Passionate Problem Solvers on the Court

"One of the greatest values of mentors is the ability to see ahead what others cannot see and to help them navigate a course to their destination."
John C. Maxwell

As a coach, what is your greatest joy? Is it seeing your player win a match? Or is it seeing your player employing a philosophy you helped foster to confidently change the course of a match, thus showing his or her love and respect for the game? While each coach approaches this answer personally, we want to suggest that the best way to create tennis players for life is to ensure they understand completely the problem-solving aspect of the game.

One the greatest joys we find as coaches comes with seeing players get the point of strategies and drills in such a way that they incorporate those strategies and drills into a whole approach to the game, as opposed to using them just to win a particular match. Great players live for every moment of the sport and love the big moments whether they win or not. Players in basketball, football and hockey love the pressure of hitting the final homerun in the bottom of the ninth, catching a touchdown pass with only seconds on the clock, or taking the game-winning shot. It is no mistake that the game's greatest players understand, embrace and respect the problem-solving aspect of the game, which takes discipline, focus and hard work. Roger Federer has said, "There is no way around the hard work. Embrace it."

Novak Djokovic, as a very young player, grew up learning tennis initially in the bottom of an empty swimming pool in war-torn Serbia. Djokovic once said about Roger Federer and Rafael Nadal, "Roger and Rafa have been so dominant that to compete with them has been difficult. But it is also a challenge. Every time you play them they make you improve," which shows Novak's love for problem solving. His whole career he has thrived on how to improve against these players instead of focusing on when he has lost to them.

As coaches, we are called to do more than teach players how to hit an inside-out forehand or a slice backhand, but also to love under-standing why and when they should use them. Tennis players have to understand they are playing a sport that involves problem solving every time they are in the moment of the point. The best ones love everything—which spin to hit when, where to place the serve, what racquet to use, where to hit the return, etc. They are never tired of being students of the game because they know failure comes with thinking they have no more to learn. Here are three basic principles you can use to inspire in your players a desire to be problem solvers on the court: **purpose, perseverance and philosophy**.

Purpose

One of the best ways to ensure purpose in a player is to create purpose in the warmup of a lesson, whether it be private or group practice. From the first ball, players need to hit with purpose, focusing on the following progression: height (net clearance), spin, depth, direction and speed. For example, as players are warming up service line to service line, have one hit topspin and one hit slice, and give them a goal of a certain number of shots and then alternate. As they are hitting, encourage them to figure out how to deal with these different spins. In addition, make sure players demonstrate purpose in their shots based on their understanding and execution of various situations—defensive, neutral or offensive.

Perseverance

Perseverance is defined as continued effort to do or achieve something despite difficulties, failure or opposition (www.merriam-webster.com/dictionary). Great athletes of all kinds, especially tennis players, possess this quality in order to problem solve in their matches. It's important for us as coaches to create a desire in our players to focus on all parts of a match, especially those that require the hardest work mentally, tactically and physically. One way to do this is to have servers only get one serve, start a match down 0-2, or one player can only hit slice backhands. In other words, make sure your players face many different scenarios that will help them understand how every single point counts. Tennis is one of the few sports where match problem solving has to be done by players themselves with coaches providing only a road map for various situations. Unlike in other sports, tennis players on the pro circuit cannot turn to the bench to get advice when they are in trouble in Grand Slam events.

Philosophy

Now that your players have purpose and perseverance, ensure finally that they have a sound philosophy when they play matches. Many players go out and just play without adhering to a certain philosophy. However, as coaches we have the responsibility to provide a basic philosophy for our players that allows them to handle anything they may face, both on and off the court. Below are some of the main points we believe are important for such a winning philosophy:

- Remember the reason for playing tennis goes beyond winning or losing a match.
- Revel in the moment to determine one's own destiny on the court.
- Never forget your strengths and know you will always have them no matter what the opponent does or what happens in the match.

Again, ask yourself what is your greatest joy in coaching? What are your players' greatest joys in playing? Our hope is that these simple principles will help you create problem solvers on the tennis court and lifelong players.

Four Foci of Student Retention

> "I love the winning, I can take the losing,
> but most of all I love to play."
> Boris Becker

> "I play each point like my life depends on it."
> Rafael Nadal

As coaches we want our students to continue to come back for lessons. While this is a fine goal, we have found that the main goal should be to have your students continuing to play the game of tennis. The best way to achieve this playing retention is based on four foci – **improving students athletically, mentally, competitively and socially.**

Before we delve into the four foci of student retention we want to share some research about juniors and adults on **why they play sports**. Take note that **winning** doesn't play much of a role in the research. In an article by Mark Hyman (1/30/2010) from the *New York Times* titled "Survey of Youth Sports Find Winning Isn't the Only Thing," he cites the following finding from what Michigan State researchers Martha Ewing and Vern Seefedlt concluded in 1989 from their study of 28,000 boys and girls around the country on "Why you play sports?" He explained the top answer was "fun" followed by "to do something I'm good at" and "to improve my skills." The answer is "winning" did not crack the top 10.

A study done by researchers at the Harvard Opinion Research Program and the Hard T.H. Chan School of Public Health in partnership with the Robert Wood Johnson Foundation and NPR (June 2015) found that among adults' top reasons for playing sports are personal engagement (55%) and to improve health, get in shape or lose weight (23%).

Athletically
   Students, whether kids or adults, want to make sure they are athletically challenged in an environment where activities are not too hard or not too easy. The goal should be to find the "athletic balancing point" that brings out the best athletic performance in a student. We have found this approach helps create responses such as "Let's do it again!" or "That was fun!" This concept can be applied to any age and athletic ability level. The truth is players will more likely continue to participate in activities where they can be athletically successful. This can be as simple as two young children tossing a ball across the net or adults doing medicine ball tosses along the baseline with a partner.

Mentally
   Players want to improve tactically as much as or more than they want to improve technically. We have found that our most successful classes occur when we are able to understand how to help players develop the mental side of their game. So we work to apply it to our coaching in a way that players feel challenged and inspired. We don't want to coach players who just perfect their ground strokes. We want our players to have the street smarts of the pros mentally, tactically and strategically.

Competitively
   Students want to be competitive in some way or another when they play. A great coach understands and implements the level at which any game should be played. This means that regardless of what the score is in a game the player has the capability to compete against any opponent. Great coaches understand that it is their responsibility to set the environment that fosters this approach to competition. We have found a great way to start lessons is make sure the athletic warmup portion of the lesson includes competitive games. The Z ball warm up challenge is a great example of a tennis specific competition without using either racquets or tennis balls. Kids especially love this game.

Socially

Players participate in sports for all kinds of reasons, but especially social reasons. They range from playing with their friends, wanting to find new players within their sport, wanting to get a good workout with other people, or seeing it as a great way to practice with fellow team members. Whatever the reason there is always a social aspect involved and it is the coach's responsibly to figure that out. We have noticed the most highly attended events have a main theme tied to them whether it be around a major pro tournament, a family theme (parent-child) or a charity fundraiser that helps foster a social connection for all players involved.

So finally, do you want to retain your players? Then allow them to improve **athletically, mentally, competitively and socially and they will come back for more!**

Keys to Coaching Champions

"Our chief want in life is somebody
who will make us do what we can."
Ralph Waldo Emerson

"You know you do need mentors, but in the end
you really just need to believe in yourself."
Diana Ross

How do you coach players to play like champions? The answer revolves around one main concept—telling players, "You can do it!" when they think they can't, and helping players believe they can be the champions they already are.

We both have had the honor of coaching USTA Mid-Atlantic teams at the summer Zonal L2 Level tournaments. During the tournament, we coached one of the two groups of top players (both boys and girls) from the Mid-Atlantic section who were competing against the other top players from other USTA sections. The atmosphere of this tournament is exactly like a college match. We have had some amazing coaching experiences through this tournament.

One of those experiences included the Mid-Atlantic team that was successfully battling its way through to the Championship final as one of the two undefeated teams in the tournament, only to end up two matches short of winning the final round. After being down six matches in the doubles, this particular team, however, won the singles round 8-4. Although not quite enough to win the whole thing, it was an exciting comeback to the very end!

The coaching that week was based on the following principles:

Allow the Players to Understand and Implement Your Coaching Philosophy

There are three areas the team focused on from first practice to last match: **1) play smart mentally, 2) have fast feet, and 3) compete!**
Every player showed all three.

    1. **Mental Focus** - Player's ability to focus on areas in their control, regardless of winning or losing the match

    2. **Footwork Focus** - Player's ability to apply correct footwork fundamentals, based on the situation on court

    3. **Competitive Focus** - Player's willingness and belief to compete on each and every point, regardless of the score

Tell the Truth and Inspire

One of the players Jeremy was coaching had won the first set in his singles match. He said to his player, "Great job!" However, he also said to him, "Expect your opponent to start playing better, and not to expect to play perfectly yourself." Jeremy reminded his player, "It's all about percentages. You will make mistakes, but know you are still in control." When Jeremy's player was up 3-1 in the second set, he served and hit a great approach forehand that set up an easy backhand volley, which he proceeded to hit wide, thus losing the game. During the changeover, Jeremy's player said, "Well, Coach, I made the easy mistake you said would happen, but I am still in control." Then he proceeded to go on and win the second set and the match.

Know Your Players

During the tournament, we would have at least six matches going at the same time, and it's pivotal that a coach know what each player needs. Just knowing which players liked reassurance, which wanted specific tactics, who needed emotional support and not much coaching at all, was vital. For example, we had our players that were in three-set matches and down in the third set focus on one tactic and told that player, "You are a champion!" during every changeover. So, knowing exactly what to tell each player individually has been crucial to our teams' victories.

Listen to Your Players

In the first round of the tournament, the Number One boy won the first set but was down 5-2 in the second set. During the changeover, Jeremy asked the player, "What do you think is his weakness?" Jeremy and his player figured out together that his opponent was weakest moving forward and dealing with different paces. So, Jeremy told him to start hitting two slices short in the court and one topspin to his weaker side. He executed this strategy perfectly, came back and won both the set and the match. By totally frustrating his opponent, the player got back into a winning mindset. When he came off the court after the match, he said, "Coach, you are the reason I won that match!"

Always Instill Belief in Your Players

Great champions fight 100% of the time, whether ahead 5-0 or down 0-5. They fight when they are up 5-0 because they respect the other player's ability and assume their opponent will start playing better or never give up. They fight when they are down 0-5 because they want to walk off the court knowing that every moment of the match they gave their absolute best to win.

On the night of the doubles portion during one of our teams' finals match, our team was feeling good, because we had tied or been ahead after all our doubles play to that point. But unfortunately, that night, we lost every single doubles match and were down 0-6. The other team only needed 4 out of the 12 singles to win overall. The next morning, when we played our singles, our match was at 8:00 am. The team got there at 7:15 am to practice and warm up. Jeremy let them know that today was a new day and that we still had a chance to win. He was able to do two things that really made a difference in the outcome.

1. In his pre-match meeting, Jeremy turned to each player individually and addressing each by name, Jeremy said, "You are a champion and you will win today!"

2. Jeremy also had the top boy and the top girl on his team give a little pep talk to their fellow players about not giving up and fighting to the end that day.

The team went on to win 8 of the 12 singles matches and fell only one match short of causing a deciding tie-breaker match for the overall Championship.

In conclusion, what have we learned from coaching in this incredible competition? We learned to communicate clearly our coaching philosophy of **focused mind, fast feet** and **compete, to tell the truth**, and **inspire, to listen** to our players knowing their strengths and weaknesses, as well as what gets them going, and finally, **to help them believe in themselves**.

Mental Metrics for Evaluating Players

"The fifth set is not about tennis, it's about nerves."
Boris Becker

"Tennis is mostly mental.
You win or lose the match before you even go out there."
Venus Williams

This chapter is for everyone who plays tennis—world-class pros on the circuit, college varsity athletes, nationally and state-ranked juniors and seniors, and all those club and league players who tear up the courts year after year. It even includes Bud Collins' "hackers." Maybe the players you are coaching picked up tennis later in life, like later than sixteen, which means they've already passed their prime for winning Wimbledon. But they're very serious about their game and work hard to improve it. They take lessons and record all the major tournaments on the Tennis Channel then watch them religiously. They are often seen sparring with a ball machine after lessons with you. They may even be spotted on airplanes carrying at least two racquets in search of a game on the road. On the NTRP rating they are between 3.5 and 5.0. The purpose of this chapter is help. This chapter is for coaches who want to use ***mental metrics*** in their teaching.
    Great coaches' help players **think beyond how they are hitting their shots** to how they are preparing to play, **how they are handling the stress,** and **how they are** actually **playing the game mentally and emotionally.** One way for coaches to do this is to teach players to evaluate themselves on several levels which goes well beyond their level of skill.
    This technique of evaluation comes from Jeremy's father, Dr. William Carl who provided the information for this chapter.

His findings also come from observing the Lavers, McEnroes, Lendls, Borgs, Connors, Everts, Navratilovas Beckers, Edbergs, Federers, Nadals, Djokovics, Williams sisters and Murrays, all of whom he has seen play in person and on television. His conclusions come (with a PhD in Communication) from analyzing and evaluating all kinds of people, helping them perform better whether it be in public speaking or sports.

Tennis, like any other sport, is a complex activity that involves a whole range of abilities that include but go well beyond the level of physical skill. As Timothy Gallwey in his **Inner Game of Tennis,** James E. Loehr in his **The Mental Game,** Skip Singleton in his **Intelligent Tennis,** Allen Fox in his **Think to Win,** Brad Gilbert in his **Winning Ugly,** and more humorously Simon Ramo in his **Tennis By Machiavelli** have shown us, tennis involves so much more than physical skill. Club and league players, and incidentally world and junior champions, who understand this difference are the ones who usually come out on top especially in tight matches.

Since the spring of 2000, Jeremy's dad has been lecturing on the Brain at medical schools and medical conferences all over the country and internationally as well. His lecture offers a philosophical/ethical perspective on the Mind/Body equation with some of the latest information on neuroscience. His research in neuroplasticity has contributed to developing some of the ideas in this chapter in addition to helping Jeremy be an even better player and coach.

So, the question you might be asking is how can coaches help players take their game to the next level, and even a level beyond that? The answer is help players develop the ability to evaluate themselves on a 10 to 1 scale (10 being the highest) in the following areas:

Artistry, Brains, Confidence, Experience, Fun, Focus, Inner Peace, Intensity, Preparation, and Stage Fright.

You might even want to call these the **ABC's** of *the serious tennis player.* If players can be honest about themselves in these areas and do specific evaluations with your help after playing their matches they can begin to put the spotlight on the places in which they need to improve. They don't have to score a perfect ten in every area to win or even to have a good time playing. None of us is perfect, not even the top ten in the world. However, what your players want to do is to make as high a score as they can in all of these areas. But first they have to be aware of them and how they play themselves out in their personalities. What these **ABC's** provide is a different way of charting your players' matches that is very precise.

ARTISTRY This is the level that has to do with one's skill as a player. Some players seem to be born with natural talent. It seems like they hardly need any lessons. They just pick up the racquet and hit the ball the right way and do amazing things on the court practically from the beginning. They never seem to be off balance or out of control. Their racquet seems to be an extension of their bodies. **Timing and flow** come naturally. **Speed, quickness,** and being in the **right place** at the **right time** are all an effortless part of their games. Ken Rosewall always had this kind of **balance**, timing and flow. But I am also talking here about sheer genius where names like Laver, Goolagong, Nastase, and McEnroe immediately come to mind. It may be a surprise to the players you coach but they have more of this raw talent than they realize. All those lessons with you should be trying to draw the best out of them, the artistry that is unique to them and their games. After each match evaluate the skill of your players' shot-making, their balance, timing, flow, and speed and then give them a score of 10 to 1 on the Artistry scale.

BRAINS There is, of course, no substitute for intelligence in any sport, but especially tennis. Players need to be thinking all the time about their game plan, sticking with it as long as they're winning and even when they're losing if their opponents are having a hot streak that just can't possibly last. What we're talking about here is **playing smart.** Think how many times coaches have seen club and league players blow matches just because of dumb mistakes in shot selection or strategy. We've seen players who score higher on the Artistry scale lose to players with less skill but more "court smarts," which sometimes even happens at the national and world class level as well. Some players just **figure out ways to win.** They just seem to have the ability to size up their opponent's weakness and attack it relentlessly, almost boringly, or they take their opponents out of "their" game by not playing into it. Ashe did exactly that against Connors the year Ashe won Wimbledon. Of course, Brad Gilbert is a great example of this kind of **street-smart tennis** even if sometimes by his own admission he used to play "ugly" (thus the name of his book with that title). It may mean remembering to help your club or league players to spin their first serve in at crucial times instead of blasting it, not switching to serve and volley suddenly if they are winning from the baseline or something as simple as throwing up a good, deep lob the next time the opponent charges the net instead of going for that "needle-threading TV passing shot" down the line. **Playing smart** also means being **alert**, constantly looking for a place to take advantage. It means **seeing** several shots **ahead** the way great chess players do by seeing early on the pattern of your opponent's shots and remembering that under pressure that favored pattern will emerge. After their next matches score your players 10 to 1 on the Brains scale and then ask them, "Where and how specifically could you have played a more intelligent match?"

CONFIDENCE   There are some players who walk onto the court with such a **winning attitude** that it shows in everything they do and say from body language to facial communication to the way they warm up. You just have this feeling about them from the beginning. They mean to win. There is no question in their minds. What gives them such confidence especially against players who may be ranked higher, have more skill and experience and are by all rights supposed to win? Are they born with it or have they learned it somewhere? We think it's a little of both. Borg, Connors, Navratilova and Evert always had it, Seles and Courier both had it and Federer, Nadal, Djokovic, Murray, Wawrinka, Zverev, Thiem, Dimitrov Serena, Halep, Pliskova and Sharapova have it today. Every time they take the court you just have this feeling they're going to win. Perhaps that's in part because every time they begin the warm up they look across the net and say quietly in their own minds, "I am going to hit the ball over the net one more time that you are," and then they do it. John Wooden who coached UCLA to more NCAA championships than anyone has ever done developed confidence in his players by demanding that they master the basics, the fundamentals. He didn't have them watch films of opposing teams. His theory was to be so good yourself that it doesn't matter what the others do; they have to adjust to you. Now that's confidence! Which is **not cockiness** although a touch of that is not bad. The problem with cockiness is that it's always born in insecurity and nervous fear and often collapses under pressure or explodes when things don't go its way. True confidence in your players is a **belief in their own powers**, respect for their ability and an ever-present image of themselves as the great players they are becoming. It means trusting in themselves, knowing what they can do and then doing it, in other words, **being the best they can be**. Confidence comes in part from the encouragement and cheerleading of coaches like you who are "for" them, but **ultimately it has to come from within**. In tennis confidence comes when your players believe in themselves completely then practice and play with such **consistency** that they are ready for whoever and whatever comes. Just bring them on! **Winners play with confidence**. Losers don't. That's the fine line between them, especially in amateur tournaments. They may still lose but it won't be because of a lack of self-assurance. Stan Smith and Billie Jean King were great models of what I'm talking about. You can help your players if you begin giving them a grade of 10 to 1 on the Confidence scale after every match they play.

EXPERIENCE can be a wonderful thing—that is depending on what kind of experience you have had. We've seen club or league players with twenty years' experience lose to players with only four or five. Why? Because the ones with twenty years' experience had never changed. They still hit the ball the same old way. They had never developed their game. In fact, all they had was one year's experience twenty times over, or worse, twenty years of bad experience—lots of bad habits grooved to perfection. Have you ever asked a player after a match, "What went wrong out there?" and the player had absolutely no idea what to say? In other words, they hadn't **learned** anything **from the experience**. Experience can be a **great reservoir** from which to draw if (1) your players **pay attention to what is happening**, whether they are winning or losing, and even when they are getting drummed off the court ask themselves, "Why am I getting beat? How can I prevent this from happening the next time by working on this or that?" (2) your players take on lots of different types of opponents (pushers, serve and volleyers, all-court specialists) especially outside their club or league, so your players actually have the experience of playing different styles and thus are more ready for whatever comes in their club, league or team matches and then are not surprised and thrown off by something they've never seen before, and (3) your players **pay more attention** during lessons with you to improve in a specific area and then try it out, win or lose, in their next matches. We know some players who "hit" with their pros every week but whose game never seems to change, not because of the pros, but because they never learn anything from the experience. Remember, "it's what you learn after you know it all that counts!" The pros on the circuit understand, that's why they all have coaches helping *them* learn from *their* experience. As you evaluate your players on the Experience scale and give them a grade of 10 to 1 following match play get them to answer this question: "Did my previous experience make any difference in that match and did I learn anything at all that will help me play better in the next one?"

FOCUS may be the hardest thing for a club player to maintain. Even world class athletes like Becker, Ivanisevic, and Korda used to lose it in Grand Slam matches. As the Aussies like to say, their minds "went on a walkabout." Others call it "La-la" land. It's like our bodies are playing the match, but our minds are someplace else. Actually, focus is **both mental and physical. Mental** focus means complete mental concentration. It means not letting your mind wander to what's happening at the office or the joys or trials of a certain relationship or the in-laws coming to dinner or anything else. One thing about snow-skiing is that it demands your complete attention, especially if you're going down a black slope. If it doesn't you end up in the infirmary. The same should be true of tennis. The world may be coming to an end, the pro shop may be burning down, but you don't even know it because your mind is completely on your game at that moment and it stays that way to the very last point. Machiavellian opponents will try to throw you off at the change-overs by bragging about your serve or telling you how you used to stink but now you don't or general chitchat about the stock market or whatever. That's a very old trick and it even works! Maybe you've tried it in matches you've played. But it won't bother the players you're coaching because their minds are unalterably **centered** on the match and nothing else. **Physical** focus is on the ball: where it is at all times, how your opponent bounces it before the serve, where it's tossed, how it sounds as it hits your opponent's racquet, how it's spinning as it comes across the net, what it looks like at the moment it meets your racquet and how it spins as it crosses the net and reaches its destination, the exact spot you had in mind. Think about a camera having to be in focus before a photographer can take a picture. Your players are that photographer getting **everything in focus** and keeping it there **from beginning to end.** At first they start out in manual focus and it takes a little longer to **concentrate.** As your players they learn to move quickly to *automatic focus* where they don't even have to think about it; so the next time your players break their opponent's serve, they keep their focus up by winning their serve and closing the door on their opponent. The by-product of focus in tennis is **consistency** which **equals winning every time**, especially at the amateur level. It means never beating yourself again. Borg, Connors, Evert, Courier, Seles, Chang, Serena, Djokovic, Federer and Nadal have all won a lot of money and fame by keeping their tennis cameras in focus. After each match evaluate your players' performance by giving them a grade of 10 to 1 on the Focus scale.

FUN Club or league players who take themselves too seriously, can't **smile** at their mistakes, and don't have a good time just playing the game, usually get too uptight, which leads to more errors and eventually defeat over and over again. Tennis is a wonderful game full of rhythm, poetry, symmetry and sheer beauty. It's a real joy to play whether you win or lose. Obviously, it's more fun when you win, but we love just hitting whether it's in a match, a drill, or a warm-up. Seles and Graf enjoyed it so much they could hardly wait for the ball to come over the net so they could smack it again. Have you ever seen anybody enjoy tennis the way Jimmy Connors used to? He absolutely loved the game which then led to his **creativity** and **gutsiness** even in tough matches. He just let go and had a good time. When players that you coach are having fun playing they can even **do something wild** occasionally when they get on a roll like actually going for a winner! Fun is the alter ego to the more conservative Focus that wants you to make sure you hit every ball in. If focus is the prefrontal cortex of your brain (the brain's parent), fun is the limbic system (the brain's teenager). This doesn't mean getting giddy on the court. It just means helping your players "lighten up." Fun here doesn't mean the social element of just being with your friends or playing social tennis (which usually drives most serious players crazy). No, fun here means the enjoyment of competition and the sheer delight and pleasure that comes with achieving excellence. Serious players who can combine fun with a little artistry, brains, confidence, experience, and focus have a great time and often win more than they lose. They revel in the sheer kick of competing. Evaluate your players on the Fun scale and give them a grade of 10 to 1. This one may be the easiest one to evaluate for most coaches. Good coaches know which players are uptight and which ones aren't.

INNER PEACE Many people were impressed with Timothy Gallwey's **Inner Game of Tennis** when it first came out back in the early 1970s. It was accompanied by an atypical videotape. Perhaps it was his more philosophically Eastern way of thinking and approach to life that caught everyone's attention, all that "Zen and Archery" or "Zen and the Art of Motorcycle Repair." Whatever it was players began *painting pictures* of the path of the ball in their mind's eye before they hit it and then let it flow through them and watch it actually do what they had seen visually. Inner Peace means playing with complete awareness, but not thinking too much consciously about what you are doing, but just letting go and doing it. Soldiers experience this state and perform great feats with a battle raging all around them. Michael Jordan used to do it with thousands of NBA fans sending up their deafening roar. Some call it **being in the zone.** Some call it **being at one with yourself and your sport**. Whatever you want to call it when you get into it you can actually visualize yourself hitting every ball in and then doing it. It manifests itself in **poise** and **composure, ease** in any situation no matter how difficult. When you attain this state of inner peace, your **temperament** is right which means you never lose your temper. Players love it when their opponents lose it because they know it will throw them out of the "zone" and they can close in for the kill. When you play with inner peace, you never fight against yourself. One opponent is quite enough. You certainly don't need two. Edberg and Sampras were great examples of players who seemed to achieve a high level of inner peace time and time again. Worked for them. It can work for the players you are coaching. Pay attention to your players' level of Inner Peace and give them a grade of 10 to 1 after every match they play.

INTENSITY Since so much of tennis is psychological, it's important to remember that one of your goals is to break your opponent's spirit. Some players actually give up before the match is over. Some give up before they start. "I can't beat this player, so why try?" Your goal is not to be that kind of player even if you're down 6-0, 5-0, 40-Love. **You never give up!** This can unnerve your opponent. Chang and Connors did this to everybody they played. Nadal does in every match. They never give up no matter how bad it gets. Why? Because they have the desire to win that is born in intensity. You have to want to win to win and intensity is what gets you to your goal. Intensity comes from deep inside you. Players who have **snap, zip, competitive drive, fire, fight, enthusiasm, hustle,** and **second effort move their feet**. Players who don't, don't. The opposite of intensity is flatness, lethargy, and sluggishness all of which lead to sloppiness and defeat. *Victory is not handed to you on a platter. You have to earn it and to earn it you have to want it.* Intensity can buy the players you are coaching at least one or two points per game. In a close match that's all they need to win. Develop the skill now to evaluate the players you are coaching more specifically by giving them a grade of 10 to 1 on the Intensity scale.

PREPARATION "Preparation, not possession, is nine-tenths of the law," said the Law School professor to a class one day. **Practice, practice, practice.** Since **consistency with authority** is a key to winning most amateur matches and 95% of them are lost due to inconsistency, practice for ruthless consistency is crucial. Practice "kick" second serves until you can hit them in your sleep. Practice early preparation. Practice the 4-by-4 drill where you and your practice partner hit the ball 4 feet over the net and 4 feet inside the lines every time and hit it as hard as you want. Lendl and Navratilova started aerobic exercise off the court at least three times a week working out with a few light weights, pushups and sit-ups. Now every top player is a fitness fanatic. When I began doing that years ago my game improved by 30% to 40% since I could move faster, hit harder and stay out there longer. The best coaches show their players how to practice **with intensity** and to practice correctly lest they groove bad habits. Practice makes perfect only if you practice perfectly! Good coaches remind players that they should never let a ball bounce twice in practice or they will do so in a match. Your players need to practice getting into the state of **inner peace** even during a lesson, while hitting with a friend, and especially with the ball machine. They shouldn't waste a single second hitting sloppily and should keep their **focus** up on every shot throughout their practice or not practice at all because **the way they practice is the way they will play!** Learn how to evaluate your players on the Preparation scale by asking yourself, "How well was this player prepared for this match?" then give that player a grade of 10 to 1.

STAGE FRIGHT Greater than the fear of death or any of the other many phobias lurking about in modern society the fear of embarrassment is the greatest one of all which is one reason so many people have so much trouble getting up and speaking in public. The same is true for athletes performing before others even if the only "other" is one's opponent. The important thing to remember is that everybody has stage fright, even Broadway and Hollywood actors and actresses and Presidents of the United States. It doesn't really matter who you are. We all have stage fright. If you don't, you're either dead or you have no business being in front of others doing whatever it is you do. The trouble is Stage Fright can hit tennis players at the most inappropriate times, like at Love-30 or in close tie-breaks or when they're serving that second serve with set point against you and as Bud Collins likes to say, "The concrete flows through the elbow." Or it can often happen when you're ahead and trying to close out a match. The important thing to remember is that there are **two kinds of stage fright: nervousness** and **excitement**. Nervousness means that you aren't prepared and thus not confident in what you are about to do and have a right to feel nervous. Excitement means that you are prepared, confident and ready, and you just train those butterflies to fly in formation. You channel that excitement into doing a great job, i.e., playing at the top of your game. Stan Smith believes that having this **little edge of nerves** at the beginning of a match is a good thing. Without it, if you're too relaxed, you'll be flat. Sometimes it's helpful to identify the fear specifically. Fear of what? Losing? Winning? Not looking good when you play? Embarrassing yourself in front of other players? Why worry about any of that? You're going to do what you're going to do. If you're

prepared, playing smart, confident, focused, ready to have **fun** and not take yourself too seriously because of your feeling of **inner peace** and **intensity**, you're going to be the best you can be and thus **have nothing to fear**. Of course, all good club and league players know that bouncing up and down a little between points and as they wait for the serve and "moving those feet" during points does wonders for getting rid of the jitters. Evaluate your players on the Stage Fright scale after each match asking yourself this question. "How did this player handle the anxiety and stress today?" and then give that player a grade of 10 to 1.

Once you have learned to use all of these mental metrics in evaluating players' performances on the court, you can help them work specifically on what is holding them back from winning their matches psychologically. After each match add up all of a certain player's scores and you will have that player's grade out of 100. But more importantly you will have begun to identify with great precision the specific areas where that player needs to improve. If the overall grade was below 50, that player probably needs improvement in all areas. If it was 70 or above, but one or more of the areas scored below a 7, those are the areas where that player needs the most work. If your player scores 80 or above, and played an opponent of equal skill level, chances are your player won that match handily. Ideally, you will teach your players how to evaluate themselves in these ten areas because unless your players are on a high school or college team, they won't have you as their coach out there with them when they play their matches. Eventually they are going to have to figure out how to win all by themselves. So, helping them learn to give themselves grades in these areas will actually help them be the best club, league or team players they can possibly be. And that is the greatest gift a coach can give a player—the game of tennis for life!

Here is an evaluation of Jeremy after he'd played a championship match in a tournament in Texas when he was 16.

Evaluation of Jeremy Carl
Dallas Labor Day Open
Round of 16 – September 4, 1993
Won: 6-4, 2-6, 6-2

	Grade	Comments
Artistry	8	**Great form on volleys** and half volleys; super work on bending knees; great slice backhand – much better than last match; your top-spin backhand is getting stronger all the time (how about match point!); **you showed better form on forehands** than last time except when you lift up and the ball flies long; only real weakness on form was overheads when you didn't move and point at the ball
Brains	7.5	You stuck with your attacking game well; **good approach shots** especially on slice down the line – very sharp! and consistent; you attacked your opponent's weaknesses well through a strong serve and volley game and consistency

		on ground strokes in the 1st and 3rd sets, especially the 3rd; you are still closing too tightly to the net leaving you susceptible to the lob; you only left the forehand court open twice – see if you can eliminate this mental error and buy yourself two points in the next match by scrambling more quickly back to the center of the court after each wide backhand
Confidence	7	Great confidence in 1st and 3rd sets! But too much show of dismay in the 2nd set which gave your opponent confidence, something you never want to do; keep acting like a winner particularly in the warm-up
Experience	8	Same; your experience in serve and volley match play is paying off!
Focus	7.5	Great focus in 1st and 3rd sets; **never let up** after you win the 1st set; you eliminated double faults and increased consistency on ground strokes except for the 2nd set
Fun	7	Overall **you had fun,** but you got down on yourself too much

		in the 2nd set or you would have scored a 9 here; I did see you smile a few times – way to go!
Inner Peace	8	You are such a **natural, talented serve and volleyer** that you were **"in the zone"** throughout the 1st and 3rd sets but even looked good on S and V in the 2nd set. The "zone" went away on ground strokes in the 2nd set but returned in the third, especially in the way **you remained completely calm** with your passing shots when he came to the net; **you seemed to "see" your shots going in every time** in your mind in that third set which added to your confidence
Intensity	8	**Good intensity level;** lots of fire! Hustle! And drive! Especially in the 1st and 3rd sets; you were much more **stingy** about giving up points and **greedy** about winning them except in the 2nd set; the only place you need more intensity is in "moving your feet" and "pointing" on overheads – think Roadrunner!

Preparation	7.5	Much better preparation this time; **good discipline** in practice, adding the work out at the fitness center helped your strength, speed and endurance; good focus on your **positive mental attitude** except in the 2nd set; you had much better preparation on ground strokes; **outstanding last shot of the match with an awesome topspin backhand** that landed in the corner which will give you tons more confidence on this shot in the future
Stage Fright	8.5	You **didn't appear nervous** at all; your increased confidence kept you calm and positive on crucial points, all of which you won handily!
Total Score	77	Your serve/volley game was stronger and your ground strokes were much more consistent; you also won key points in 1st and 3rd sets; you **kept your focus up after breaking serve** which shows improvement in your game; great match! Keep your goals before you and keep working hard; you're on your way!

The Perfect Lesson

"You have to believe in the long-term plan you have but you need the short-term goals to motivate you and inspire you."
Roger Federer

Now that we have laid out the reasons to coach, skills needed to coach and goals for coaches, we will touch on coaching philosophies and guidelines for creating the perfect lesson. One of the most fulfilling parts of a tennis coach's day is finishing a lesson and hearing from your student, "That was perfect!" Without even asking the student, "How was the lesson?" the student has voluntarily communicated that he or she enjoyed the time on the court. You have provided that person a great experience, not just a lesson. It is not the tips students are paying for but how the pro communicates the tips in the lesson that are important.

This approach can be achieved based on two principles (a) being passionate about what you are coaching and (b) caring that your students learn. From our coaching experiences, we have found these two principles help create the "Perfect Lesson" which includes knowing what motivates your student, coaching in a situation-based environment, providing a simple and specific tool for correction for your students when playing, using all teaching tools available to help students, and being engaged from start to finish.

(1) **Knowing What Motivates Your Student**

Every student's reason for taking a lesson is different. It could be a cardio tennis drill style workout, a lesson on a specific singles or doubles tactic, a lesson on a specific stroke your student struggled with in the last match, just a playing lesson with no technical tips, a junior lesson that focused more on athletic skills than hitting or a beginner who is ready to learn anything about the game. Everyone wants to learn something but it is the coach's responsibility to figure out what that is.

Learning about student's motivation requires asking the right questions. It should follow an opened progression that leads to what aspect of the game the person would like to see improved. You could call it the pyramid method of questions where you ask general questions about the person and then continually narrow your questions. For example, you could ask these questions with someone wanting to be able to handle deep balls to the backhand side:
Question: "Tell me about your tennis game."
Answer: "I play in leagues and with friends."
Question: "Do you play more singles or doubles?"
Answer: "I like doubles but need to work on singles"
Question: "Tell me about your singles."
Answer: "I am pretty consistent from the baseline but have trouble when pushed behind the baseline to my backhand".
This type of learning environment will allow your lesson plan to be geared toward the motivations of the student and not the coach. This is especially important if working with a person for the first time.

(2) **Coaching in Situation-Based Environment**

Once you have the motivation of the student clear in your mind, you can decide how you want to train the student and practice a certain skill. This can involve baseline to baseline play, serving, returning, coming to the net or dealing with an opponent coming to the net. In the end, a player, regardless of level or age, needs to practice within a situation whether it be more of a playing lesson or shot specific lesson. The coach and the student need to answer three questions: when to use it, why to use it and how to use it. All three questions should be answered in your lesson. It's important that the coach and the student agree on which situation to practice. How much time to spend on "training the skill" will be determined by the motivational reasons the student is taking the lesson. For example, the person who wanted to work on the deep backhands might want to make this part of the lesson only 10% of the time and the rest 90% playing.

(3) **Providing a Simple and Specific Tool for Correction**

Now that you have learned what motivates the student and figured out a situation to practice, next comes creating a learning environment, not a lecturing environment. This is crucial to any productive lesson or tennis experience. As a coach, it is easy to focus on impressing a student with all the knowledge you have about tennis. However, students regardless of age or ability only want a good experience which includes learning something they can remember and use on the court to help them play better.

Tennis is a lonely sport when competing, and coaches need to help students learn how to correct their own mistakes during a match on the court. The best coaches help their students make self-corrections that are simple and specific. 'Simple' means they could explain the correction to another person in less than a minute while 'specific' means it is easily understood. One of the best ways to see if the student and you are on the same page is asking at end of the lesson open-ended questions such as "What are your thoughts on the lesson today?" or "What did you get out of the lesson today?"

(4) **Using all Teaching Tools Available to Help Student**

Once you have established what motivates students, set up the correct situations, and provided a specific and simple tool for correction, then you need to use all the teaching tools available to you to help students improve. Think about the analogy of technicians coming to fix your cable service or an appliance in your house or apartment. Wouldn't you want them to bring all the tools at their disposal to solve the problem? In the same way, tennis coaches should apply a similar commitment to their students by using every tool available to them.

Here are some examples of the kinds of tools we are talking about: If a student is having trouble visually understanding a stroke you are demonstrating, use your smartphone to record yourself hitting the stroke in slow motion and then have the student watch it a couple of times. Depending on how sophisticated your video is, you can really slow it down so the student can see where the face of the racquet is at contact. We've used this technique many times and it's amazing to see how well students contact the ball after seeing us hit it in slow motion. If you are teaching kids who like music, use a tool like Pandora to find a kids' mix of music to play while you do specific hand tossing or racquet feeding drills with them.

(5) **Being Engaged from Start to Finish**

It's the experience students want, not just a lesson when they come to you for help. This means from the get-go, you need to ensure your first activity is dynamic and 'level appropriate' but also gives you a chance to be totally focused on observing your student's athletic range by moving around as an active coach, not a statue coach. A great analogy is the energy that football coaches demonstrate when they run out on the field with their team before the game starts. Always find a positive in any mistakes made by students so that you are constantly encouraging them.

In summary, make sure you start strong and finish strong. Show your enthusiasm for how your students performed in the lesson and link what they accomplished to the next lesson. Be passionate about tennis—caring that your students learn, and you will know what motivates them. Coach in situation-based environments while providing simple and specific corrections. Use all the tools available to help students, and be engaged from start to finish. These strategies will lead you to a perfect lesson.

Point 3
Tennis Management and Leadership

Creating a Successful Program

"If you're ridin' ahead of the herd, take a look back every now and again to make sure it's still there."
Will Rogers

Every tennis teaching professional aspires to run or be associated with a great program. However, this desire may never be realized if it is missing the key components to achieve longevity. Throughout our years of teaching, creating and implementing programs we have made plenty of mistakes. In the end, we have realized the need for certain parameters to be in place in order to assure that a tennis program thrives and lasts.

Start Small

All great businesses start small. Once upon a time, Starbucks had one store, and Apple had one product produced in a co-founder's garage. The same is true with a tennis program. Quality over quantity will always breed success. Growth needs to be steady and planned. From personal experience, Tim knows the huge problems that can arise if you fail to have the necessary infrastructure in place when you make the move from running one to two clubs. Omitting any part of the crucial steps for success can create debilitating complications in the long run—lesson learned.

It's all in the plan

No program will succeed unless there is a detailed plan that can be executed and followed. Many tennis pros are part of a successful group, and when that group grows and they add a program, and then another, complications occur because this is not a plan. It is imperative that a pathway for any new program be laid out before the first ball is struck. Tennis coaches don't have to implement all the programs at the start, but they need to be diligent in adding and adapting based on a solid end goal. Successful programs always originate from a plan that has the end in mind.

The golfer Gary Player used to say that the harder he practiced the luckier he got. This same approach applies to planning in detail because it forms part of the practice culture that eliminates mistakes and allows for successes early on.

Details

A successful program doesn't happen if there is no attention to details. What do we mean by details? Well, it is imperative that a program be organized structurally, day to day, hour by hour. The more focus on the details of what will be offered to how people register and pay the better the experience will be for both organizers and the participants. Programs often fail because the details are not covered. It doesn't matter how great a coach you are or how wonderful your personality is, it will all come crashing down if attention to detail is not there. Let's highlight a few examples of what is necessary for a successful approach:

- An organized and clear pathway for all participants
- A detailed pricing structure
- A detailed and targeted marketing plan
- Detailed lesson plans and follow-up

A successful program establishes expectations for its participants and the executed plan should achieve if not exceed those expectations.

Character and Integrity

People will make mistakes, both the programmers and the clients. What keeps the program moving forward in the right direction and people lining up to pay is ultimately the character and integrity of the program. These traits must be first and foremost in the minds of all personnel from the owner to the housekeeping staff. In the same way it's important to ensure that participants bring the highest level of character to the classes—no exceptions. Participants and parents should not be allowed to behave poorly. For example, we have had experience with players who have been disqualified from an event for foul language and abusive behavior towards staff members. Other issues involve arriving late, being disruptive and even destroying property. Your program will lack the character and integrity it needs to thrive if any of these things occur without your bringing them to the attention of the players involved. If it happens on your site then it reflects on your program and your team. What we are talking about is creating a "culture of integrity" that permeates your entire organization.

The Best Program avoids Pitfalls

Here are some pitfalls your club or organization should avoid:
- Staff rosters published late;
- Consistency is a premium; watch about inconsistent pricing structures and different discounts for different clients;
- Communication via cell phones not clearly addressing clients' needs;
- Playing favorites—all clients should be treated equally; reward effort and client contributions equally;
- Problems with billing and communications generally; if mistakes occur your program's brand will suffer;
- Lack of feedback to participants;
- Participants not paying on time (after all, the financials are the essential part of growth)

Getting Bigger

The growth of a program can be exciting but needs to be subjected to a great deal of scrutiny so that mistakes aren't made along the way. As lifelong proponents of growing the game of tennis and coaches who are entrepreneurial-minded and eager to grow, we have made and corrected mistakes that could have adversely hurt not only our own growth but the growth of our staff, our participants and ultimately our program and industry reputation.

The growth of a program shouldn't be driven by the idea that "a class is full so let's add another!" Smart industry leaders monitor a growing class and then separate it into other classes to maintain quality and expectations. They also understand that the answer is not merely in the addition of new classes unless it fits the original plan and the next step in the pathway to the organization's ultimate goal for success. For example, imagine that you have a High-Performance group and the class is full. Simply adding another class to the program may work for you financially in the short-term but not necessarily in the long-term. It might seem obvious to add another class, but a better approach might be to separate the High Performance Group into different levels, which creates better quality and will increase retention. Great programs have ever-expanding pathways to incorporate all tennis players at every stage of the game and every stage of their advancement.

Staff is the most important asset you will have as you get bigger because there is only one of you and you can't do it all! We understand that financially it might make more sense in the present to add programming and to wear yourself thin doing all the lessons and clinics, but this approach will eventually have a ceiling and could lead to burn out. Always, hire, train and retain great staff so that as the leader you will also grow. For many teaching professionals running or building a program, adding great new staff is easily your most worthwhile investment. As time goes on you will reap the reward of not stretching yourself too thin and having high quality people helping you grow your program and your brand.

Trends that last

We all know that tennis is continuingly evolving and that it is imperative to stay current with programming, drills, technique, vendors etc. Thus it is important to make sure you are informed. Although it is nice to jump at every new idea, vendor product, or continuing education opportunity, DON'T. Make sure anything you do is tried and tested. Without mentioning names, we have been very eager in the past to pull the trigger on a variety of tennis related trends, then we put a lot of time and energy into them with no reward. Tennis is about consistency and therefore you, your staff and your program must be consistent from top to bottom, from what and how you are teaching to what you are selling in your shop. There is tremendous value in consistency. Look for example at the Professional Tennis Registry (PTR) and the years and years of continued growth and success it has enjoyed as a teaching organization. It is this type of consistency that creates trust and encourages the consumer to respect what is offered from lessons on the court to new racquets in your shop.

Creating a tennis program that is successful, a program that grows and ultimately lasts, is not easy. The principles we have discussed in this chapter represent some key elements you need to safeguard the integrity of your program. Remember that a program will only grow if it starts small, is nurtured with the end in mind, has a plan that can adapt and evolve while you make every effort to develop a great staff. Finally, you should absolutely love every second of the experience!

Remember we teach our students to deal with the peaks and troughs of playing a competitive match; make sure you do the same when building and running a program. Try to avoid the pitfalls and be proud of your program whether it has 5 participants or 500.

Growing and Developing your Staff

"Never tell people how to do things. Tell them what to and they will surprise you with their ingenuity."
George Patton

Imagine it is your 10th year coaching with an organization and you feel stuck in your position. You have been working hard putting in the required hours of coaching and providing fun, engaging and enjoyable practices for your students. However, you wake every morning thinking, "I have no way to develop or grow in my profession or organization or for the betterment of my students."

Our goal in this chapter is to help you create a positive work environment—one where coaches feel excited to go to work knowing they have the chance to be constantly growing and developing their skills as teaching pros.

Since we have both been fortunate to hold great leadership positions in the coaching world, we have developed some important principles on the subject which revolve around one main concept—**creating and maintaining a good culture in the staff.** Leading a successful and productive coaching staff involves first and foremost applying principles that create highly engaged people. Take note of the findings detailed in an article from the *Harvard Business Review* (May 2013, p. 100) titled "Creating the Best Workplace on Earth" by Rob Goffee and Gareth Jones.

> "Take these two examples: Research from the Hay Group finds that highly engaged employees are, on average, 50% more likely to exceed expectations than the least-engaged workers. And companies with highly engaged people outperform firms with the most disengaged folks—by 54% in employee retention, by 89% in customer satisfaction, and by fourfold in revenue growth. Recent research by our London Business School colleague Dan Cable shows that employees who feel welcome to express their authentic

selves at work exhibit higher levels of organizational commitment, individual performance, and propensity to help others."

As you can see from the above research, employees who feel highly engaged in the workplace have a profound effect on the success of their institution or company. This research shows an important connection to highly engaged people in three crucial areas—employee retention, customer satisfaction and revenue growth. In fact we like to use the following model for these three principles—employee retention + customer satisfaction = revenue growth. We have found that a working environment with both good employee retention and customer satisfaction will always lead to healthy growth in an organization. We've mentioned before how coaches are tasked with many responsibilities including motivating, encouraging, teaching, empowering, guiding and mentoring. It is virtually impossible to expect your coaching staff to exhibit the above mentioned qualities for their students if the culture of the workplace itself doesn't foster those positive qualities. Leading an effective organization is like coaching on the court or the field—people will only "work hard" if they are intrinsically motivated to do so. There is no getting around that. Motivation is probably the most human connection to a job that a person can ever have!

Look at the top ten reasons why people leave an organization in the article by Mike Myatt from *Forbes* (December 13, 2012, online article) titled, "10 Reasons Your Top Talent Will Leave You"

- You Failed to Unleash Their Passions
- You Failed to Challenge Their Intellect
- You Failed to Engage Their Creativity
- You Failed to Develop Their Skills
- You Failed to Give Them a Voice
- You Failed to Care
- You Failed to Lead
- You Failed to Recognize Contributions

- You Failed to Increase Their Responsibility
- You Failed to Keep Commitments

Before we get into the main principles that help create this positive environment, it is important as a leader of coaches that you and your fellow coaches are all on the same page when it comes to the following questions. While you might come up with more yourself, we believe these questions are very important to the success of creating and maintaining a good culture in the staff and helping deal with some of the ten reasons why people leave a workplace.

- What describes a good culture in your staff?
- How do you define success for your team?
- What is good customer service for your members or students?
- How do you celebrate the successes of your team members?
- How do you value and listen to the ideas your team finds important?"

While every coaching team has to establish its own common answers to these questions, the best answers revolve around each member of the team respecting each other's views and working toward the same goal in order to grow the organization.

Now that we have touched on the overall principle and the important questions teams must ask themselves, we will examine the key principles that create and maintain a positive team culture. These are principles we've developed from our years of experience.

Creating a Culture of Ideas and Inspiration

Our leadership experiences in coaching have taught us that the fostering of ideas and inspiration are crucial to any successful coaching staff. The best way to create a positive environment for your students starts with setting a positive environment for your coaches through ideas and inspiration. This feeling of inspiration and creativity will then be translated from coach to student on the court or the field. Inspiration and creativity always unlock the passions of the coach. A great head coach or head pro is able to foster a creative environment so that other coaches feel free to share their ideas. Just as we believe coaches should be proud of their "brand" and the "added value" they can bring to their students, in the same sense, each work culture should have a "brand" that they are proud of and is evident through the actions and attitudes of its coaches. Every work culture is defined by a "brand" that is attached to it whether they like or not.

Coaches who aspire to make coaching their career usually view this future career as their "dream job." While we certainly agree that coaches should view their positions as "dream jobs," the wrong culture can be a major deterrent for achieving this view and lead to "burn out" or "feeling stuck in one's current position." This can cause coaches to find themselves in a "dead end job," and certainly not their "dream job."

Developing this kind of positive work culture starts with ensuring that creative ideas are encouraged from your coaches and never discouraged or downplayed. It starts with letting people be themselves and embracing the diversity of the passions and personalities within your staff. It involves finding ways to motivate coaches to unleash their ideas. Below are some main strategies we have found successful in helping coaches release their creative side.

- Ensure that during scheduled team meetings new ideas involving all aspects of your sports industry are encouraged. This could be off the court ideas that involve marketing, business, charity events, crossover sports and partnerships ideas. While working at an athletic club, we found that some of the most well attended and well received events for members at the club involved multiple sports or athletic components.
- When deciding on new program ideas or classes for your club or organization, provide monthly or quarterly opportunities for any member of your staff to propose a

new program, including all aspects of it from pricing to promotion.
- If doing super clinics or special events at your club finds each coach taking ownership of a certain topic to present to the members, you will energize your coaches to generate more ideas for future clinics or programs. One of the most successful events we had at Mount Vernon Athletic Club in Alexandria, VA was holding "Member Grand Slam Super Clinics" around the time of each of the four major Grand Slam tennis pro tournaments. We always had music and food included in the event. Participants would rotate courts with a pro doing a specific game or drill on each court; then the participants would play round robin or the same game on each court after that. This format allowed each coach to focus on a topic he/she was passionate about.

Public Praise and Covert Criticism

One of the most important management techniques that will help you create a positive work environment is public praise and covert criticism. This means you offer public praise for coaches who have made the effort to improve and refine their coaching skills for their students through professional development of some kind. Also it's just as important to provide constructive criticism about each coach's performance but always privately, never in front of others. In fact, a good critique of another's performance should always begin with something positive then move to how the person can be even better. In addition, we have found the best ways to provide public praise are through member newsletters or social media. When doing this ourselves, it is has been amazing to see the unleashed productivity and passion displayed by our coaches.

In the end, we have found that all the raises or title changes in the world will not encourage employees to stay unless the team culture encourages, values and recognizes coaches emotionally and not just financially. We have found this to be very true especially when a coach is just starting out with a club or organization and looking to make those connections to build his/her lesson base. One of the most powerful things you can do as a head coach is to show your new coaches that you understand this point and care that they succeed. Remember that coaching involves the business of making connections, and coaches have to be encouraged as they are building those connections with students. For example, in the same article from *Forbes* by Michael Myatt, he mentions that when employees were interviewed, "more than 70% don't feel appreciated or valued by their employer." While changes in titles or increases in compensation play a significant role in a positive workplace culture, they are not the only important factors in employee retention and productivity.

In summary, growing and developing your staff revolves around creating and sustaining a work culture that allows this to happen. So ask yourself this question and then answer it: how are you fostering a positive team culture among your coaches?

Providing Opportunities

"If your actions inspire others to dream more, learn more, do more and become more, you are a leader."
John Quincy Adams

Are you a tennis pro or a tennis entrepreneur? In this day of constantly competing ideas and challenges to our industry, it is important that tennis pros be more than just tennis teachers. They also need to tap into their *inner entrepreneur*. Tennis pros should think about themselves as *a brand* and constantly audit themselves by asking such questions as:

Who am I?

Where am I in my career?

Where am I going and what do I want to be?

How do I get there?

Tennis coaches should be like leaders in any profession. Leaders have two qualities: confidence about their product or skill and passion for passing along their knowledge beyond the four walls of their club/organization. They are also never satisfied with the number of people who are using their product or service and know that there are always more ways to grow their product.

Spreading the game of tennis requires establishing an emotional connection with students, which is a major component in creating financial growth and stability. Remember that it is not until your students realize how much you care that they will also begin to understand what and how much you know about the sport. At the end of the day, it is not how many people you know, but how many people want to know you.

Once you have established your brand and people know your value outside the four walls of your club, the next step is to be proactive. In the book *The 7 Habits of Highly Effective People* (Simon & Schuster, 2013) Stephen Covey suggests the first habit of great leaders is to "be proactive." One of the best ways to be proactive comes from creating opportunities for your own and your pros' professional development, and tennis playing opportunities for your students and prospective tennis players.

Creating Opportunities for Your Professional Development

Below are some ways you can create opportunities for your own professional development:

- Take advantage of the many continuing education courses.
- Offer free (eventually fee-based) high school seminars for high school coaches in the area and present on topics that appeal to them. We know from personal experience that this is one of the best ways to help gain more confidence in your coaching, increase exposure for you as a coach and, most importantly, spread the game of tennis.
- Post tennis tips through social media or club newsletter.
- Submit articles to the various magazines in your coaching area.
- Donate coaching lessons at charity/non-profit organization auctions or events.

Creating Opportunities for Your Pros' Professional Development

Tennis directors or head tennis pros should not only care about their players' development but also care deeply about their coaches' improvement. All coaches have a story to tell about their tennis development, and it is important that we assist them in helping shape and improve that story.

Be a model to your pros by:

- Making yourself accessible

- Opening yourself up to ideas and suggestions
- Getting excited over staff success—celebrate with and for them
- Include your pros in the goal-setting process by educating them on revenue goals for the department. Do not forget to explain why and how their goals are tied to business growth and profit so that they can feel included as part of a bigger picture.
- Create incentives and ownership opportunities for your pros. Encourage creative ways for pros to attend continuing education events. For example, take away the cost barrier to attending these seminars. Provide a goal (revenue or sign up totals) for specific programs that they are leading. If they reach their goals, then the organization will pay for registration costs or other fees associated with attending continuing education programs like these.
- Provide low cost, monthly super clinic nights for your members. Allow each pro to do drills/games on a topic for which they have a specific niche or passion. This allows members to come together as a group, make friends, and create a more tightly-knit community.
- Encourage your pros to create player development resources for their students by having them perform player assessments for students at tournaments, Junior Team Tennis matches, or after each clinic session. Player development should be a two-way conversation with coach and student, not just coaches telling their students what to do.

Creating Opportunities for Students and Prospective Students

In addition to helping create a proactive culture in your club that facilitates entrepreneurship and ambassadorship among you and your fellow coaches, creating playing opportunities for your students and prospective players is equally as important.

Think about these opportunities:

- Offering coach-supervised match play classes in addition to the regular classes. For example, we offered match play dates for our orange and red ball classes. It was great to see how kids and parents embraced it. One way to make tennis as attractive as other sports is to offer "play days;" similar swim meets for swimming and game days for soccer. It is important to be as creative as possible when offering tennis play options to students of all ages and levels.
- Encouraging and creating Junior Tennis Teams (JTT) for all levels and ages of play in your program. One of the most rewarding ways to initiate a kid's love of playing is to set up 8-and-under red ball JTT teams at your club.
- Reaching out to all the local public and private schools in your area, even if they do not have tennis courts, to offer 10-and-under tennis in their gyms. This will help expose kids to the game and will allow them to be more involved in your tennis program during the summer.
- Offering to host a USTA YoPro event geared towards attracting more young professionals to tennis. It is a fun event for ages 18-39. It includes round robin play, corn hole, ping-pong as well as food and drinks.
- Offer programs to students who are homeschooled in the community. This will benefit those students who, unlike their counterparts attending public and private schools, would otherwise not have exposure to sports in the same capacity. In addition, it will help get those kids introduced to such values as sportsmanship, physical balance, athletic skills, and stress management.

So finally, as a tennis coach are you creating your brand and your story, establishing an emotional connection with your students, and being proactive in creating opportunities for your development, your pros' development and your students' development? If so, you are on your way to finding the inner entrepreneur in you that is spreading the game of tennis!

Point 4
Tennis as a Business

Collaborations—Working as a Team

> "My mentor said, 'Let's go do it, not 'You go do it.'
> How powerful when someone says, 'Let's!'"
> **Jim Rohn**

Economists analyze the USA's economic activity as the total demand generated by consumers, businesses, and government. In a similar way, tennis activities also include an incredible mix of consumer activities, business, and government investment. We should ask ourselves on a regular basis and at all levels of the sport "is that incredible mix operating to its maximum potential?" The key to this mix is clearly the understanding that, underlying all sport, is a partnership structure that provides investment in required facilities and equipment, the regulatory structure that facilitates competition and, most importantly, participation for all ages and ability levels.

At a local tennis level, your community club will probably present a mix of outdoor and indoor tennis court activities. In addition, your community club will present activities in a gymnasium or swimming pool and classes (individual or group) focusing on fitness, strength, and stamina. The average participant, a player or parent, should not spend time considering how such an operation achieves its "go to market" standard – an action plan that specifies how a company will reach customers and achieve competitive advantage. However, a quality management team would spend considerable time planning, implementing, and monitoring such a standard.

It all starts with People

All salespersons, at some point, have been told: "people sell to people." During a time where the internet runs consumerism and business practices, there may well be many exceptions to this view. But in a service economy based on customer participation, it certainly applies. In a tennis club, "people" will consist of patrons/members as well as club staff. However, to achieve that attractive offering that sets your club apart from other clubs, it will also include investors, sponsors, professionally trained coaches, related contractors/businesses that provide in-house services (e.g. offering catering or refreshments to club members while they are using club facilities), equipment and apparel from well-known brands (i.e. Wilson, Head, Nike, Under Armour), and small companies that provide other auxiliary services such as water dispensers or air conditioning. All of these groups contribute to making a club successful. If one part fails, then the club will perform below its full potential.

As a consequence, all club managers need to identify stakeholders that provide or facilitate elements of its service and ensure that appropriate "partnership" agreements are in place to secure successful performance. Ask yourself, "With whom are we currently partnering?" and then ask "who would you like to partner with?" When the answers are the same, make sure there is a partnership agreement in place that achieves your goals. Where the answers are different, evaluate why and ask how to transition to an appropriate partner.

Partnership Approach

In a sports business, partnerships can be found at many levels. Many businesses would have the traditional Board of Directors, Executive Management team etc. But in many sports clubs you would also find a "Management Committee" that would consist of business executive leaders as well as Men's and Ladies' Captains and selected members that would help to develop the Club from a member's perspective. In addition, there may be formal or informal associations, with titles like Affiliates, Advisory Committee and Alliance, which contribute to the shape and governance of the sport in that location/region. These associations do not emphasize the business aspect but are nevertheless critical for developing grassroots competition, access to a broader base of participants, and partnership with local institutions that benefit from such participation (e.g. schools, colleges and local councils).

Reasons for partnership from a club perspective can be business oriented in that they contribute to revenue growth, increase member participation, and improve customer retention. Other reasons for partnership include enhancing reputation (targeted marketing, selection of court surface with infrastructure supplier), utilizing in-house marketing of club activity through a regular newsletter, and supporting club environment (e.g. making sure the club parking lot is well lit to support family safe environment). In addition, partnerships can also be about community engagement. Because local governments and local communities seek to promote healthy living by increasing physical activity, tennis can contribute to achieving that objective. What is crucial in all of these efforts is the recognition that a successful partnership should be a win-win relationship for both parties; only then are such agreements are sustainable.

When reviewing this wide range of partnership opportunities, key factors such as club brand, values, and standards should be considered then shared with potential partners and featured within the final agreement. This will mean both parties can monitor performance, provide information as required, and determine the level of resources and supporting processes needed. For instance, an upmarket exclusive club might not host large participation events but would probably want to link with Professional Tour events in its area as a way of reinforcing its brand strength. Alternatively, a family orientated membership would find extra activity within school vacations attractive.

Partnership Identification

Having decided to enter into a partnership, the next steps would be these: (1) identify existing relationships and then (2) evaluate the existing performance and partnership structure. This stage reflects a transformation program that needs you to determine your vision, values, and objectives, and then evaluates which partners are best suited to achieving those goals. In some situations, the actual partner choice may surprise you (i.e. a partner that is hungry for your business may offer better services than your previously assumed choice); in other cases, it may not even be a commercial agreement. Remember in the tennis world, we may be discussing participation with volunteers, local government, or non-profit operations where there is an umbrella type agreement and the club provides "activity" under the patronage of the local government/non-profit organization or with the support of volunteers. Remember that it is this mix that makes our sport special.

Successful Partnerships

If we look at the range of partnerships a typical club could have we would expect the following categories:

Club Member/Management relationship
Employee/Management relationship
Facility Management
Sporting Goods/Apparel providers
Local Tournaments to advertise Club offering and enhance membership numbers
Local and Regional United States Tennis Association
Community Participation in Local Government, Schools, Vacation programs etc.

Each of these categories requires assessment as to the club's value and its objectives. That assessment helps you determine the level of resources, reward structure for employees, and partners and then required processes and information flow to manage the business. Across the board, there has to be a win-win philosophy to make the business a sustainable success. Achieving a consistent approach that blends innovation and cost-effectiveness to the level of demand for a given location requires partnership agreements to be scalable and in place. This includes collaborating with partners to contribute to the identification of issues and solutions. It is often said in the outsourcing world that the best contracts are those where the combined team does not need to refer to the contract.

The approach to partnerships of "start small and think big" is applicable. Within a tennis club, each aspect of the operation contributes to the success or failure of the total. Your tennis court infrastructure may be the best that technology can provide, but if the experience with the reception team, quality of the changing rooms, and pre-court drills are not up to standard then the overall experience is less than desirable. "Start small" in this context means that even the smallest detail needs management focus.

To reiterate the approach that "it all starts with people," in a service sector business, which tennis is, people can become supporters, ambassadors, donors, investors and much more for your business. Relationships on all levels are your greatest asset. Such an asset needs to be developed and managed on a truly win-win basis.

Vision for Tennis

Tennis is often grouped with a number of other sports that competes to capture the public's attention, strives to increase participation, and capture market share. To achieve this goal, tennis as a sport needs success at the highest level but also at the local level to ensure availability of courts, ease of entry to participate, and a social attractiveness across all age groups. If this is our vision, then partnerships are needed to secure that investment and that appeal. Should not every school have a tennis program that feeds through to the college and adult level? With this in mind, what partnerships will you develop in the future that will enhance the great sport of tennis?

Tennis Entrepreneurship

"Do not follow where the path may lead.
Go instead where there is no path and leave a trail."
Ralph Waldo Emerson

Entrepreneurship is a primordial urge to identify and fill a need and is independent of product, service, industry or market. The business of tennis is similar to the game itself since a businessperson must adjust his/her strategy and think creatively to be one step ahead of the competition. Through entrepreneurship, one can create a more personalized approach to the sport of tennis, publicizing one's specific uniqueness, while at the same time having a positive impact on the surrounding community in a sustainable manner.

Personality provides a vital component to business growth and development distinguishing successful companies from others. Entrepreneurs should share their stories telling who they are and where they are from, creating a sense of emotional connection with the company, which can lead to increased financial stability and growth. Coaches who have a more intimate connection with their company and their audience are not only better able to understand what their business needs to grow, but also inspire others through their passion. As the old saying goes, "People don't care how much you know. They want to know how much you care!"

In order to begin building a brand, an entrepreneur must first establish a strong network of professionals, possible clients, and partners. This task should not be taken lightly, as this is the basis of support for building any business. If one support structure falls, it is imperative that another be reconstructed, so as to avoid the collapse of the establishment. Business networking should include advisors, preferably those with experience, who are able to guide the company as well as provide expert perspectives about business decisions, ways to expand, and publicity.

While it may not seem like it, taking advice is actually a skill, and it is one that entrepreneurs need to develop through their involvement in the business world. Ignoring the perspectives of others remains a colossal pitfall for many businesspeople. It's a practice that may create a reputation of recklessness or rudeness while, on the other hand, taking advice from everyone without discretion may show signs of weakness or hesitation. However, respecting others' opinions with a discerning eye involves more than just being polite; it is an essential part of making informed business decisions. Entrepreneurs need strong viewpoints while also being able to understand different perspectives in order to become successful.

Running a business is not easy, and it never will be, which is why it is important for coaches to understand what their motivation is, whether it be fame, fortune, passion, or giving back to the community. We should never lose sight of our goals since there will be certain obstacles or rough patches that will require gargantuan amounts of time and effort to overcome. For example, paperwork and legalese can be time-consuming and mundane and may make entrepreneurs question their motives for starting a business in the first place. However, it is actually okay for entrepreneurs to be absolutely obsessed with what they do, and it is a quality that can be used positively to conquer hardships that often arise in business development.

Once the business is established, it will need publicity. It doesn't matter if somebody has the absolute best tennis programs and state-of-the-art facilities; if nobody knows about it, there is no way that business can stay above water since there are no customers. Marketing is arguably the most effective way to publicize, and one of the biggest mistakes new business owners can make is to overlook advertising as a means of attracting customers. It also requires a strategy and purpose; nonchalantly putting up flyers will not bring in any new business. It is important to understand who the target audience is as well as the most effective way to advertise to that particular group of people.

Companies also need a steady stream of revenue to stay in business. Investments and sales are typically the most common means of funding, and both are intrinsically linked. The popular TV show Shark Tank portrays this connection perfectly. One of the first questions asked by any of the potential investors is usually related to a number of sales the company has generated, and their biggest turnoff to investing is a lack of sales. Even if a certain product or service may seem like an amazing idea, an investor needs a quantitative measurement that indicates its ability to create profits. In order to attract investors, a business will need sales, which is not possible without marketing.

Think about the hundreds of different pizza delivery chains or soda companies. Although they sell the same type of product, there are distinct differences in the branding of the product. Some people prefer Pepsi over Coke, and some may prefer Papa John's over Domino's, or vice versa. Although there are slight differences in the way the products are prepared, maybe one type of pizza seems less oily, or one soft drink is less acidic than another, the biggest distinction is the brand associated with the product. Perhaps one of the best examples of this is the phenomenon known as the "Pepsi Paradox." Even though more people say that they prefer Coke over Pepsi, in blind taste tests, the same people that prefer Coke actually select Pepsi as their preferred beverage. Sometimes, branding can be even more important than the quality of the product, and while quality is still very important, associating a particular product or service with a positive message helps popularize that product, service, or business.

In the modern world where social media dominates all other means of communication, it is crucial for businesses to use it properly. Whether for work, school, entertainment, or countless other possibilities, people are constantly using the Internet, and so it is important to establish an online company image through multiple social media outlets that are commonly used to market to as many people as possible. Another great benefit of social media is that it is extremely cheap compared to other means of marketing. The only potential cost is paying an employee to keep social media updated, but there is no direct cost in updating profiles and uploading photos to the Internet. It also takes a minimal amount of time to maintain since it can be done practically anywhere, making it very convenient for an employee to work from home. Not to mention, it is less intrusive than phone calls, less expensive than mail, and less annoying than pop-up ads.

Finally, run the business as if it were a Fortune 500 company. Structure is a vital component to managing a business, and so businesses should have clear and concise policies, especially those regarding customer service. Nothing makes a person angrier than a grumpy and unhelpful employee in the customer service department. This is why companies need informative training for new employees as well as an established hierarchy. Bureaucracy is typically perceived negatively, but the concept associated with red tape and endless rules and regulations, however, is only true in ineffectively managed bureaucracies. Regulations and policies help to level the playing field so that all customers are treated equally and are necessary for the management of any business.

Tracking Trends and Increasing Profits

"In God we trust, all others must bring data."
William Edwards Deming

"What gets measured gets managed."
Peter Drucker

Imagine you are in a typical office space. Look around you—there are patterns everywhere you can see. Perhaps it is the plain stripes on the carpet, the ugly tiled ceiling, or even the usual clutter of your workspace. Now that those patterns have been identified, what will you do about them? Do you clean up the clutter or not? How much time and money would it take to make these changes? Is it worth it? Essentially, informed business decisions work the same way—identifying patterns and using data to support conclusions.

Collecting data takes time and effort spent through surveys, e-mails, and other means, so why bother? Let's look at one example in particular—Walmart. If Walmart, a company averaging more than $470 billion dollars in revenue, could more accurately predict customer spending patterns by just five percent, Walmart would generate over *$23 billion more*. I think it's safe to say that the effort of collecting data is worth it.

Data analysis is by no means new. As a concept, it has existed since ancient Egypt, where a census was required for the building of the pyramids. More modern means for collecting data were invented in the 1890s with the creation of the Tabulating Machine, a punch card system of storing data, and today we have computers to take over the meticulous processes. If data analysis isn't new, then why has it only become used recently?

In one word, the answer is **leadership**. For example, the movie *Moneyball*, a movie about the birth of modern baseball statistics, accurately depicts how professionals believe that expert opinion outweighs data. Billy Beane, the manager of the Oakland A's, realized that athleticism did not win games; it was the runs scored that mattered. He proved the methodology of data analysis through winning 20 games straight, even with a very constrained budget.

Tennis is no stranger to data analysis; in fact, it has become increasingly common in recent years. Rather than solely for professional use, such as the statistics that appear on the TV screen after a set, coaches have begun to use statistical measures for analyzing a player's shot selection and consistency. In fact, it is generally more effective than traditional coaching methods, as players are able to better visualize areas of improvement through the expression of data.

The real takeaway from the application of data analysis to sports is that quantitative observations always beat out qualitative. In fact, one experiment proves this by taking 87 Harvard law professors and pitting them against a statistical model with six variables to see which side can more accurately predict Supreme Court cases. Of course, the model won. Opinions are always biased, but data never is. That is why data is always more accurate than opinion.

In order to analyze their market better, businesses group customers into similar areas. There are three ways to do this: clustering, network analysis, and text mining. Clustering means measuring similarities between customers, including purchasing patterns, location, and demographics. Network analysis distinguishes how customers are interrelated. Text mining is analysis of social media and other online means and extracting what the customers want. Once this is done, a statistical model can assign predictive scores based on data from past experience.

In today's competitive business world, data analysis is a necessity rather than just a benefit. As shown by Walmart's revenue example, the use of data properly makes an enormous difference, and revenue-generating techniques such as these are never passed up by corporations. Practically every large company or corporation uses data analysis; so it has become a baseline standard for businesses, which is why it is important that companies take the time to understand and apply this technology.

Data analysis is a useful tool for businesses that want to identify their markets more accurately. It can be utilized to generate profits by accurately marketing to specific groups of customers. Businesses that use data analysis successfully are able to understand their target markets better, which eventually increases their annual revenues. All of this is true for coaches building businesses in all kinds of sports.

Point 5
Family Values

A Parent's Perspective

William J. Carl III, PhD

Okay, I admit it, I love tennis so much that as soon as our older son, Jeremy, could stand on his own two feet I put a racquetball racquet in his tiny hands, hung a tennis ball from the doorway by a string between our large entryway and our dining room and said, "Hit it, Jeremy, hit it!" Poor kid just stared at me. When he did give it a try and missed, I said, "Keep your eye on the ball!" at which point he took the ball and placed it directly on his left eye. I love how kids are so literal about everything.

Amazingly, he went on to be an NCAA All-American and Captain of his college tennis team at Presbyterian College in Clinton, South Carolina. Later, after working several years at The White House, Jeremy became a full-time teaching pro coaching at Regency Sport and Health Club in McLean, VA, the Arlington, VA and Bethesda, MD YMCA tennis programs, has served as Director of Tennis at one of the nation's major tennis clubs in Washington, DC, Mt. Vernon Athletic Club in Alexandria, Virginia, and is now a teaching pro at Belle Haven Country Club.

Jeremy was chosen as one of only 48 coaches worldwide (every 2 years) to participate in USTA's prestigious High Performance Coaching Program in Boca Raton, FL. Having completed that elite training program in January 2015, he has been certified by the USPTA as a Specialist in Competitive Player Development. He's also been selected for other High Performance Coaching programs at 2016 Indian Wells, CA and during the 2016 Davis Cup matches in Portland, OR and the 2017 Davis Cup matches in Birmingham, AL. He was also named USPTA Tennis Pro of the Year for 2016 in the Mid-Atlantic Conference, an honor voted on by his peers and he has reached the Elite Professional status in USPTA.

How did he make the transition? I wish I could take the credit, but the reality is Jeremy's game took off the moment I got out of the way. Oh, sure, I showed him a few things in those early years when he was little. But, at some point, I realized that, even though I'm a pretty good player myself and Jeremy was amazingly patient with all my parental exhortations and interventions, I was not the person to help his game blossom and flourish. Who helped me see that? A couple of pros in Dallas, Texas—David Redding at Northwood Country Club and Jack Newman at Fretz Tennis Center. Both of them showed me how to be a good tennis parent.

David Redding (who is now the Head Coach at Harding University in Arkansas) was giving Jeremy a lesson one day and I was pacing the sidelines like a caged lion occasionally growling things like, "Jeremy, move your feet! Turn sideways on those overheads! Hit that ball down the line on that approach shot, not crosscourt!" At one point, David said, "Jeremy, why don't you pick up these balls; we'll hit again in a minute," then sauntered casually my direction. I didn't even see it coming. In retrospect, I realize what a tightrope pros walk when they confront enthusiastic parents. If they turn them off, the angry mom or dad just leaves the club or finds another pro that will let them yell at their kids from the sideline.

David was very gentle with me. He simply smiled and said, "Hey, Bill, why don't you take a break and go have a cup of coffee." "But," I replied, "don't you need me here so I will know what to work on when we have practice sessions in between?" He shook his head and said something I will never forget. "It's like life, Bill. Sooner or later, you have to let him go and let tennis be something 'he' wants to do, not something 'you' want him to do. Actually, the same is true about everything in his life." Well, the proverbial ton of bricks couldn't have hit me harder. But, it was exactly what I needed to hear. I did go have that 'cup of coffee,' and it was the best coffee break I've ever had.

Jack Newman is a Master Tennis Professional and now Head Coach and CEO of the Austin Tennis Academy. He and I were talking one day as dozens of Dallas' finest junior players were going through their paces in one of his famous Fretz Tennis Center clinics. We were discussing the idea of what the parents should do and not do in order for their children to thrive in tennis. I listened carefully since Jack has sent more teenagers on to the college and professional levels than any other pro I know. I figured he had found the secret. What he told me that day actually applies to parent-child relationships in every part of life and, as David Redding had indicated earlier, not just in tennis. He helped me understand that the T-Shirt shouldn't say, "Tennis is Life: The Rest Is Just Details" but instead "Life is like Tennis: Learn All You Can!"

Jack told me that day that he's observed four types of tennis parents: **High Positive, High Negative, Low Positive, and Low Negative**. He then asked me which type of parent I thought was behind his most successful juniors, in other words, the players who went on to the college and professional levels. Surely this was a trick question, and I was right, it was. My initial answer, of course, was High Positive since I figured that High Negative, the 'yelling-screaming-kicking-things,' parents would only destroy a child's fragile ego and Low Negative, the 'simmering-on-the-sidelines-frown-faced-arms-crossed,' parents would be little more than slow-drip torture for the son or daughter slugging it out on the court. Thus, it was plainly obvious, by their names if nothing else, that High Negative and Low Negative Parents were poison for their children.

So, High Positive had to be the right answer. That was my choice and I was sticking to it. "Is that your final answer?" said Jack. Nervously, I replied, "Yes, I'm sure of it…at least I think so…." Jack smiled, going in for the kill. Wrong, tennis ball breath!

The correct response was Low Positive. What? I obviously needed an explanation, which Jack happily provided. High Positive parents hover way too much. They are too overly enthusiastic, always praising, always pumping their kids up, and always congratulating them when they hit a good shot or win this game or that match. The problem comes when they don't provide the over-the-top response. Kids get so conditioned to hearing it and expecting it when it doesn't come they are crushed. Or they feel bad about themselves because they have let their parents down. That's the hidden danger of being a High Positive parent.

Low Positive parents, on the other hand, are genuinely supportive but allow their children to make tennis their own. They don't watch every lesson or clinic, hanging around, exploding like High Negative parents or simmering on the sideline like Low Negative parents. Instead, they encourage but do not push. They support but do not intrude. They drop their children off for lessons and clinics then go get a manicure, a cappuccino or work-out at the fitness center themselves. At the end of the lesson or clinic, they pick their children up and ask them how it went and how they felt about how they did. Even after a match, they don't judge or criticize. Again, they ask the child how the experience was for them. ONLY if the child asks for it, does a parent offer any advice at all and that in the context of genuine and straightforward affirmation.

Now, I realize on the surface this sounds like so much touchy-feely, 1970s cotton candy—lots of fluff with no substance. I mean where's the action plan for success, the strategic plan with key goals and target dates? Don't we pamper these millennial and post-millennial kids way too much as it is these days? How can your child ever improve with this kind of lackadaisical "everybody gets a trophy" attitude from Mom or Dad? The truth is it works. Leave the performance assessment and enhancement to the professionals. After all, they're the ones trained for it anyway. David Redding and Jack Newman are right. I observed it myself. The players in Texas whose parents ran their children into the ground burnt them out by the time they were 18, if not before.

The day I went for my famous 'cup of coffee' and became a Low Positive Parent was the day Jeremy's game took off. He went on to be the Captain of his Division II NCAA Varsity Tennis Team at Presbyterian College in Clinton, SC, helping his team win the South Atlantic Conference Championship his senior year. His coach at the time, Bobby McKee, further developed his game and his ability to teach and mentor others. And now Jeremy is a seasoned teaching pro helping me improve my game!

In addition, Jeremy and Tim have had opportunities to teach kids at the ATP/WTA Citi Open, with Wayne Bryan, the father and coach of the Bryan Brothers. And he told Jeremy and Tim "the most important thing I ever did for my boys was to guide them in what makes them happy and success will follow." And that's exactly what Jeremy is doing with his daughter, Maggie. I can say for sure that Jeremy has learned how to be a good tennis parent.

"Billie Jean King's early sport was softball; at age 10, she played shortstop on a team of 14 and 15-year-old girls that won the city championship. However, her parents suggested she try a more "ladylike" sport, and at age 11, she began to play tennis on the Long Beach public courts." ("Billie Jean King," Biography.com)

Once during an interview, King said the following about her parents' influence on her tennis career:

> My mom came to get me, and I jumped in the car and said, "Mom, mom, this is it, this is it." She said, "What do you mean *this is it*?" And I said, "I found what I'm going to do with my life. I'm going to be the number one tennis player in the world" And my mom goes, "You have homework, and piano." My mom kept us absolutely grounded, forever! (Interview on CBS News, Sunday Morning, September 17, 2017)

Clearly, Billie Jean King's mother was a Low Positive parent. We wonder whether or not that was part of the reason she was so successful. Well, it certainly didn't hurt.

So, if you are a tennis parent, and you want to make sure your children burn out or give up the game long before they reach their true potential, continue being a High Negative, Low Negative or High Positive Parent. Your kids will quit tennis faster than a John Isner serve. But, if you want your children to go the next level and have half a chance of being the best they can be in this wonderful game, start today becoming a Low Positive Parent and watch them take off! Speaking from experience, I can tell you this—you will be glad you did.

A Sibling's Thoughts

by Sancha Legg

This book is a testament to the fact there is some great advice out there for coaches, players, and their parents. Someone that is often overlooked when it comes to advice is the sibling. Whether a brother or sister, older or younger, a player or not, if a coach and/or parent can include the sibling in the player's journey then it can that increase participation and all the health benefits that go with it. In addition, it can improve feedback and analytical skills, endorse teamwork, promote sibling respect and more practically provide a solution for childcare. This chapter looks at some simple considerations a coach can make to enhance the experience of the sibling and therefore the whole family unit. Everything mentioned below I experienced or witnessed myself. I was an active, younger sister to my brother, Tim who was a very successful junior tennis player. The strong bond I share with my brother, the respect I have for his achievements and the respect he has for my opinions were fostered through some of these simple steps.

I will start with one I am always shocked that I don't see practiced more: allow the sibling to sit at the side of the court during private lessons. However, I would a caveat here that the sibling has to be old enough to be able to sit by him/herself for 60 minutes and not be disruptive. As the coach, you should give the sibling an objective task like counting and noting the number of unforced errors, or balls in the net vs. balls played long. At the end of the lesson ask for the fact-based feedback. By being objective instead of subjective the feedback will not be taken in the wrong way. The sibling has provided a service to the player and the coach and while doing so has, in very basic terms, learned analytical skills, the importance of attention to detail and more importantly a deeper investment in your client's progress. This works brilliantly with younger siblings who aspire to garner the respect of their older siblings. The younger sibling is now the analytical coach, the person with the stats and, as we all know, information is power. The sibling is now part of the team! At the dinner table that night they can update the family on the player's progress. These lesson analytics can evolve into homework. At tournaments, simple spreadsheets can be printed off and filled in by the sibling. The sibling is entertained and not just aimlessly sitting or running around. Siblings are practicing mathematical proficiency and without knowing it learning the intricate tactics of the sport. They are being educated. Education in sport is what breeds participation and can be the simple solution to improving the gender and socio-economic gaps that sadly exist in most sports today. If siblings play the same sport themselves then they have stats to beat, mistakes to learn from and a hero to emulate.

    I was fortunate enough to go to the same school as my older brother. As any younger sibling will tell you the elder sibling sets a path to which you follow (or in my case try to beat!). My brother was Head Boy, I wanted to be Head Girl. My brother got 4 As, I wanted 5. You can only follow the good if you witness it. My school cottoned on to this at an early stage. The older kids always sat at the front in assembly, being well behaved. We wanted to be the older kids so we copied them. Fortunately, our sports club did the same. Tennis squads were timetabled so the skill set above you played on the courts next to you. There was a hierarchy of skill sets and the path to success, to the top squad, was clear. I got the same feeling watching the Top Squad girls come onto the court after I'd finished, that I did watching Steffi Graf walking out onto Centre Court. The cool thing was that the Top Squad was only a two-hour time slot away from me and an achievable shorter term goal. I often think many potential champions fail because the gap between the Top Squad and being the professional is too vast. If only there were more squads in-between. If logistics deem the same time or back to back sessions impossible then why not invite younger siblings or less advanced players along to watch the top squads train. Run a five-minute feedback session at the end. Who did the spectators think tried really hard? What did these players do that you don't do in your squads? Do you want to be in this squad one day? Yes! Feedback skills, tick. Goal setting, tick. A bunch of inspired youngsters, tick.

Finally, as a coach take time to find out more about the siblings of your client. What are their interests? This is vital if the sibling doesn't play the sport as well. If, however the siblings are active, perhaps play another sport, then find training exercises that benefit both your clients and the siblings' sport. Do both sports rely on hand-eye coordination? Do they both need upper body strength and stamina? Set fitness homework that can benefit the whole family. If siblings are not active then what do they like? I remember as a child, our family getting our first camcorder and I was obsessed with making music videos. My brother's coach suggested that I film him playing matches. Something real to film! I have never been so excited to watch my brother play a match. I remember one of my fellow player's sisters was really into fashion design and could be seen sitting at the side of the court taking inspiration from all the players around her and sketching her latest sporty designs. Do they like to cook? How about suggesting some nutritious protein snacks for your client to try mid-match? After all, I bet they are fed up with the same old boring banana and energy drink.

It seems crazy to me that so much time and effort are put into keeping parents, players and coaches focused on creating a champion and yet a key pillar to the household is overlooked—the siblings! The steps above are small, they take little effort but can transform a player's experience, the relationship with brothers and sisters and their development emotionally and educationally. Small price, big payoff. Seems worth it to me.

What Parents and Kids Both Want from Tennis

"Ill can he rule the great that cannot reach the small."
Edmund Spenser

One of the most rewarding aspects about coaching juniors is coming off the court with your junior student and the parent asking his/her child "How was it?" and the child responding "It was fun!" Then the parent says to you, "Thanks for a great lesson." The reality is every parent and child is hoping for that good tennis experience from every lesson. For many coaches this is the main motivation, certainly the first motivation for coaching kids. However, it is very easy for a coach to get caught up in seeing the kids' "potential" and start preparing them for the pro tour.

The reality is the coach, the child and the parent should work as a team with each person having an important role for developing the student. The coach is the mentor for the child on his/her tennis journey. The parent is the encourager. The child should be the driver for achieving his or her goals. Many of these principles come from the wonderful parent support structure that Tim and I enjoyed growing up. Our parents provided us the right environment to love the game then encouraged us and got out of the way of the coaches who were developing us as players. One philosophy that guided our parents was this: "Life is Like Tennis: Learn All You Can and Never Stop Learning."

Below are the main qualities that kids and parents are looking for in a lesson. These principles apply to players from ages 4 to 17. They include **awareness, valuing player's time, good communication, integrity and commitment.**

Awareness

Awareness is a vital part of what parents and children are looking for in lessons. Here are items every coach should keep in mind:
- Coaches should be aware of the child's schedule; has the child come straight from school, is he/she dehydrated, hungry or tired?
- Does the child know what skills to practice in between lessons and how to achieve goals?
- Listen to parents but be honest with them and base all training recommendations on a performance-based plan not "potential." This will let parents know you are interested in developing the whole player and help them better understand the process needed to achieve the child's goals.

Valuing the Player's Time

Parents and kids are busy. So the unprepared coach looks like the uncaring coach to both the parent and the child. The coach should respect that both the child and the parent want to get away from the regular aspects of life or need an outlet. The child and parent want the coach to know them by name. All players have similar stresses related to tennis, and the coach is there to help guide them. Time is valuable, so coaches have to be disciplined in how they use their time on the court. Coaches should always be organized, pro-active and encouraging.

Good Communication

We like to use the 90/10 rule when it comes to communication. 90% of effective coaching comes from non-verbal actions such as eye contact, facial communication and body language and only 10% is verbal. When children come off the court, parents rarely ask the child first, "What was the tip you learned from the coach today?" Instead it's always more focused on "did the child enjoy the experience and have fun?" The only way for the parent and the child to know that information is if the delivery of the lesson plan was competent, creative and concise. We have found that those three C's are the benchmarks for creating good communication in lesson.

Integrity

Parents and children are looking for integrity in their coaches during a lesson. Integrity builds respect as coaches model it for their students especially when it is a key feature of their teaching philosophy. One of the primary results of this philosophy is that it lets the parent and child know one of your major goals is to increase the self-esteem of the player. Self-esteem serves as the basis for any player's ability to compete. Some of our greatest experiences as coaches came from players finishing matches and both the players and the parents knowing that regardless of situation the players had confidence to compete on every point.

Commitment

Commitment to helping a child reach his/her full potential as a player is a vital trait that both parents and kids expect from a coach. The effect of successfully doing this equals a sports person who participates well and spends a lifetime enjoying the sport. In mathematical terms PP+CC = CSJ (positive parent + committed coach = continuing sports journey through life for the child). There are several ways a coach can show commitment:

- Focus on learning about the player first by asking these types of questions first: "What do you like about school?" "Tell me about your friends." "What other sports do you play?" "How was your camp you went to last week?" "How was your dance recital?"
- Understanding all little things matter. Being on time, prepared 15 minutes before the lesson with all the teaching equipment out. Actively listening to child's name first time. If the child is using the wrong size racket then advise the parent that the child needs to use a different size to ensure the child enjoys the game and develops correctly
- Positive and Productive Words Matter. Finding the good with sentences like "You tried really hard then, well done,

but if you could move your feet a little quicker to short balls, it will help you be on balance to hit the shot down the line." A sentence like this will motivate the child to do better and parents will see the respect you have for their child.

In conclusion, both parents and children's needs can be met in a lesson by making sure the following principles are addressed: **awareness, valuing the player's time, good communication, integrity and commitment.**

Point 6
Mentorship

Mentors Who Influenced both Tim and Jeremy

> "I've learned a lot from mentors who were instrumental in shaping me, and I want to share what I've learned."
> Herbie Hancock

Before we touch on aspects of mentoring that are important for a complete coach, we will each explain how people in our own lives mentored and influenced us all along our tennis journey. We are fortunate to have life and tennis coaching mentors who shaped both our beliefs and our practices today.

Jeremy's Mentor Influences

As mentioned in my personal background in the warmup section of the book, I grew up surrounded by pastors, educators, leaders, and coaches. While each of these mentors taught me something different, it all comes back to one theme—life revolves around making choices based on finding your passion and philosophy for life, helping others feel more confident about who they are as persons, and always striving to be excellent at what you do. I will share some stories and principles that have helped mold my view on mentorship.

The year was 1990, I was a junior player and had just won one of my matches convincingly in a tournament being held at Northwood Country Club in Dallas, TX. I came off the court all excited and said to my father, "Dad, did you see I won my match?" He said, "Yes, that's great, but do you realize you were not being a good sport on the court?" He reminded me that even though I was the better player, I still needed to respect my opponent and the game by giving 100% with a positive attitude, being ready to play every point with full intensity instead of looking bored during the match. I will never forget his helpful comment. This experience reminded me that all competitors, whether coaches or players, can't control the exact outcome, but they can control the emotions and actions they model as players and coaches.

My dad also taught me about always wanting to excel at your passion so you can help serve others get better. This does not mean he did this by sitting me down every week as a kid giving me point by point lessons on the topic, he just lived it through his actions. My dad has proven to be one of the great pastors and experts on communication and public speaking in the country. However, while he has a God given gift for speaking, he never shied away from working to improve it. One of the main techniques he teaches in all his preaching classes is "preaching without notes." While he has become an expert at this, he did not always do it. I remember him telling my mom, my brother and me one day during his time as Senior Pastor of First Presbyterian Church in Dallas, TX he was going to commit to learning his sermon so he could preach all his sermons without notes, and thus give the congregation "his very best." This action showed me his commitment and his desire to continue to improve his craft and in so doing serve the members of the church.

Tennis first and foremost is about playing a game and learning the skills correctly to be able play the game confidently. Throughout my junior tennis career, before going to college to play, I was fortunate to be with coaches like David Redding, Tim Siegel, and Jack Newman who exemplified this coaching philosophy. These coaches also showed me their commitment to excellence in coaching. Even when I participated in 'early bird workouts' with them before school, they still showed the energy and commitment to ensure that all their students were developing correctly as players.

I also learned from my former college coach at Presbyterian College in Clinton, South Carolina, Bobby McKee, important lessons about teamwork. He always set the tone that everyone's attitude and actions, whether in practice or match play, will either help or hurt the team. He also made it clear that everyone's contribution and effort, regardless of what court they played, was of equal value to the entire team.

I have been blessed to work with several great coaches since becoming a full time coach myself. One of the main things I learned starting with Feisal Hassan, Master Professional coach and international speaker on all aspects of tennis coaching, was that coaching involves teaching the game of tennis in a cooperative environment between coach and student, which allows students to apply correct techniques and tactics in match-based situations. Through Feisal's actions as a coach and mentor, I was reminded that good preparation plus passionate coaching are the important fundamentals for providing a good lesson.

In addition, as mentioned in my initial biographical information, another mentor for me early on was Senator Kay Bailey Hutchison (presently Ambassador to NATO). During my time with Senator Hutchison, I refined my writing and public speaking skills, both vital qualities of a complete coach. While my educational background through college certainly helped me with both of these skills, my time as a young professional in Senator Hutchison's office improved these skills and increased my passion for wanting to excel in these areas of communication. Even though my father serves as a great model for me as a public speaker, my experience participating in and serving as Treasurer for the U.S. Senate Toastmasters Club, a club dedicated to helping people improve their communication skills located in the U.S. Capitol Building, enhanced my public speaking confidence and capability. My weekly involvement in this club was encouraged and fostered by Senator Hutchison and my fellow Senate work colleagues. Equally important were the writing skills that improved during my time on Capitol Hill with Senator Hutchison. I was tasked daily with writing constituent correspondences for the Senator on a variety of topics. This task improved my attention to detail, clarity, and conciseness in writing and communicating. I will always be grateful for Senator Hutchison's encouragement to improve in these areas of communication, all of which have helped me immensely as a coach, a mentor and a leader.

Also, there's another U.S. Senator who has influenced me throughout my life: Senator Lamar Alexander (Tennessee) who to me has always been "Uncle Lamar" because he is my mom's brother. I remember well when he was sworn in as Secretary of Education in George H.W. Bush's Administration. A few days after his installation in the Air and Space Museum at the Smithsonian, a friend of his, Sichan Siv, a former Cambodian refugee who also worked in the Bush Administration invited my dad, my brother, David, and me to play on the White House tennis court! That's something I will never forget, thanks to my Uncle Lamar. As Secretary of Education, he taught me many life lessons but most of all how to be a good teacher, coach and educator. I also learned from him and his bipartisan approach in the U.S. Senate how to listen to all sides, especially when you are making important decisions with your coaching staff.

Life is messy and full of mistakes similar to the game of tennis itself. Just like life, a tennis match is filled with very unpredictable situations that can only be negotiated by knowing your passion and your philosophy, and bringing both to the court. Mentors play a vital role in helping people through this learning process. Here are some reflections from two of my mentors, Feisal Hassan and David Redding.

Feisal Hassan

I was Jeremy's first mentor in the tennis industry. We had and still have a trusting, confidential relationship based on mutual respect. We both knew it would involve a definite time commitment. As a mentor, I tried to model performances for Jeremy by providing him with opportunities to observe and develop insights. I tried to provide Jeremy constant quality performance assessments. In my opinion, the best learning for Jeremy came from doing. I sought challenging tasks and pushed Jeremy to develop new skills. I specifically remember having

Jeremy be the Summer Tennis Camp Director two months into his role at the club. I feel this position helped Jeremy set attainable goals, overcoming challenges while learning techniques to manage his thoughts and emotions. I was able to help Jeremy practice these skills and provide encouragement.

I also tried to guide Jeremy to understand and develop key values like honesty, integrity, respect, confidence, responsibility, perseverance, courtesy and judgment. Jeremy kept showing progress by "raising the bar" for himself as his insights and skills increased. My mentor's relationship with Jeremy ended when he was able to operate independently, and I was able to delegate projects to him and 'let him run with it!'

Feisal Hassan, a USPTA and a RPT Master Professional, is vice president on the USPTA National Board. Feisal was also the Director of Coaches' Education and Junior Davis Cup Team Coach for Tennis Zimbabwe. Feisal was also voted in Tennis Industry magazine's prestigious "40 Under 40" list for being one of the top 40 men and women under 40 years old who have had and will continue to have a strong influence in the sport and in the business of tennis both nationally and internationally.

David Redding

I used to think that winning a trophy or medal or any award was quite satisfying and the ultimate thrill. Then I transitioned to believing that there was nothing more satisfying than finding something you are passionate about, pursuing it diligently as a youth and earning a college scholarship by doing it well, then realizing you can make a very good living for nearly four decades by teaching it to others. Such has been my blessed relationship with tennis. But recently I have found there is at least one thing that is by far more satisfying: that is finding out you had a small part in passing on your passion for tennis and making a difference in the life of at least one young player at the beginning of his/her tennis journey.

It was in the late 1980's that I was one of Jeremy Carl's first tennis instructors. As the Director of Tennis at Northwood Club in Dallas, Texas, where his family were members, I was able to spend many hours both on and off court with him, feeding him balls, barking out instructions, and guiding him to new discoveries. At the very start, I wasn't certain if Jeremy's tennis lessons were more for him or for his dad. In fact, early on I couldn't tell if Jeremy even wanted to play tennis or if it was just at his father's "urging" that he play. Slowly, yet consistently his desire to be out on court, to listen to "boring" instruction, to learn better ways to move and swing, and to practice his strokes and strategies diligently turned him from someone who just swung at tennis balls into an actual tennis player. It was quite exciting to see his development and transformation both athletically and attitudinally.

I have followed Jeremy from afar with much pride over the last 30 years. He has, like I have, followed a path that has turned tennis from a childhood hobby to a competitive passion to a great summer job and finally on to his chosen career choice. There were many others who worked with Jeremy as well when he was a junior and into the meat of his career. I certainly don't take any credit for helping him get to the lofty professional level he enjoys today. I was just a young tennis pro trying to do the best I could to help a young player keep a few more balls in the court, and do it with a smile on his face. I'm humbled and honored that you consider me one of your early mentors, Jeremy. That's better than any tennis trophy. Pass it on!

David Redding, Head Men's and Women's Tennis Coach at Harding University in Searcy, Arkansas, is an Elite Profession in the USPTA and served from 1989 to 2015 as Director of Tennis at Northwood Country Club in Dallas, Texas; he played for the Harding University Tennis Team from 1979-1983.

Tim's Mentor Influences

My life has been blessed by great mentors and influencers that have shaped my life. It is important first to understand how mentors have affected my life; a mentor is someone who deliberately or by chance has a profound impact on an individual though emotional, intellectual or career pathway. Influencers are people that you look up to, admire and learn from. Many of my influencers I have never met except through research, study, and parallels; however, it is as if they are responsible for guiding my life and career.

Mentors in my life are similar to many others: my parents, grandparents and extended family, who have set forth a belief and behavioral system that shapes my informative years and gives me a playbook to make decisions. However, as I branch out, I continue to find other people to serve as a guide. Oftentimes, these exemplars aren't obvious, and many I realized years later in reflection. However, trying to identify your mentors in real time allows you to better understand the process and allow you and the mentor a chance to better connect and develop the relationship to the fullest.

Today as I write this piece, my mentors are clear and deliberate: my uncle for guidance in life and business, my wife for direction in behavior and duty, and Christopher Hitchens, Stephen Fry and Ricky Gervais as a source of great intellect and discussion, to challenge the status quo, and to be satirical, honest, and informed.

I also find great mentorship from colleagues in the industry who have set the standard and who have welcomed me into the profession, in particular, Paul Fisher. Influencers as a coach include Darren Cahill, Brad Gilbert, and Tom Gullikson. As a businessperson, the owners and executive team at Van Metre Companies have served as an example of how to conduct business. Bill Gates, who I was very fortunate to meet and coach, is someone who literally has changed the make-up of our world through invention and philanthropy, and is a person that I look up to as an example. Sampras, Edberg, Federer, and Nadal sit high on the mantle of hero status for me as a coach and tennis enthusiast, as their abilities and passion for the sport have solidified my love for tennis.

Ultimately, the range of people that have mentored or influenced me are varied and wide; some I know, some I don't, some I seek out, while others were accidental. However, I am able to take great strength and insight from these people to become a better coach, businessperson, and human being. I challenge you all to fill your lives with people that will have a positive influence on what you are doing and will help guide you where you want to go.

This reflection is written by one of my main mentors, Paul Fisher. It gives you an idea of the kinds of things I have learned from him about being an excellent teaching pro, coach and leader.

Reflections & Perspectives on a Career in Tennis
Paul Fisher

Teaching and coaching tennis was not something that I sought. Raised in a musical family, I was going to be a music educator. But as a child, I was also athletically inclined, playing basketball and tennis mainly. When I graduated from high school, I was off to music school and never thought I would play serious tennis again. However, the first person I met at college was a French horn player like myself and a talented tennis player. We started playing and found our way onto the college team. Several years later, upon graduation, I auditioned for a military band and was accepted. This time I was off to a professional music career and thought all my focus would be on that. But once again, fate intervened. I met a couple of players and soon that turned into several advanced leagues and tournaments and my tennis career continued throughout my musical career. And late in my musical career, with the help of several other players, I was able to start a junior tennis program in my community in my spare time. This then led to a full-time career in tennis for the next 25+ years.

What I've found is that music and tennis have much in common, and directing a musical group is like coaching a team and coordinating staff in running clinics. Developing common goals, focus, hard work on technique, teamwork—both disciplines require these to achieve a finished product. Through those years, there are a number of reflections and ideas that I have on a career in tennis. Some deal with the business side, some with the psychology of teaching and coaching.

The most important thing a tennis professional should have is a commitment to teaching tennis. To be successful, I believe you have to have an enthusiasm for the sport and to passing it on to your students. In other words, a professional attitude. If you don't enjoy what you are doing or are merely out to make a buck—you don't convey enthusiasm, you don't interact with the students, you just go through the motions—<u>go sell widgets</u>! Your students will notice and soon your business will dip because they will talk to each other and the word will spread. Retention will become a problem. I saw an example of this in a pro who was routinely late in arriving at the club and in his car was pulling out of the parking lot before the end of a lesson! Sometimes you have worked 14 days in a row and are tired; sometimes there has been a complaint and you are worried about that; sometimes you are frustrated because the student isn't getting what you are trying to convey; maybe the kids are acting out after a long day in school; maybe the boss is putting on the pressure to teach more lessons. All may be valid but in this business, you have to overcome these and present a professional, positive attitude.

Relationships are extremely important in this business, both with students and members but also with your boss, club manager, owners, club staff as well as your tennis staff. This can be a balancing act as pleasing one side may elicit displeasure from the other. But by establishing good relationships with people—knowing the persons, their wants and needs, being able to talk to them in a civil way—one should be able to navigate the minefields that dot the landscape. All these people can contribute to your success or failure. The front desk staff can be very important—

they are the first persons people see or talk to when they come into your club. A negative interaction—whether unenthusiastic or no greeting, poor appearance, inaccurate information—can send that potential client back out the door. AND THAT PERSON COULD HAVE BEEN WORTH THOUSANDS OF $$$$ to you over years. Maybe that person would have signed up for weekly lessons continuously for the next few years!! Treat the front desk with respect. Make sure they understand your program, its schedule, who belongs in what class......and if they don't know, have them send that person to someone who does know! It's much more enjoyable to come to work when you have good relationships with the people working around you!

Building a good staff is very important to your success and to the club's success. Obviously, you want your staff pros to be competent teachers and players. They need to be able to work within your group, professionally and personally. And healthy relationships between the individuals can make the program so much more productive and a fun, creative environment in which to work. Someone who is out for him/herself—trying to poach other pro's students, backstabbing others—is not going to engender good feelings from his fellow staff members. Students and members can be confused and upset by these negative signals and the overall program will suffer.

I would also encourage pros to approach their lessons and clinics with a positive attitude. Some think they have to be tyrannical—constantly berating students, always critical, and punishing them with grueling conditioning drills. This attitude may get results in the short-term but it wears on the students in the long run without some positive reinforcement and encouragement. Plus it may lead to a loss of self-esteem and a lack of enjoyment resulting in students either showing poor results, leaving the pro for someone else, or quitting the game entirely.

In choosing people to work for you, give them leeway to lead, be creative, and innovate within the program. Don't be afraid to let them take the lead. It should not be a negative about you if they take over. Show them that you trust them and encourage them.

Most will enjoy more responsibility enabling professional growth. It always gave me a great deal of satisfaction to see younger pros showing confidence and taking ownership on and off the court. And when it comes to paying them, spread the wealth! They help you build up the program and in turn, make you successful, both professionally and financially. In my experience, I saw others paying bottom dollar to assistant pros and the assistants never developed loyalty to the head pro and program and most moved on in short periods of time creating constant turnover. That was not a prescription for success!

Paul Fisher is a consultant to Blue Chip Sports Management and Tennis Emeritus in the areas of Expansion and Tennis Professional Program Development. In addition to playing varsity tennis at Carnegie Mellon University, Paul has won numerous awards including the following: Washington Post All-Met High School Tennis Coach of the Year, 2010; Champion of Character Award by the Fairfax County Athletic Council, 2007; Professional Tennis Registry's National High School Tennis Coach of the Year, 2007; USTA/Virginia's State Tennis Coach of the Year, 2006; Named Virginia's State High School Tennis Coach of the Year, 2005; Northern Region Coach of the Year, 2001 & 2005; Voted District Coach of the Year in several seasons.

Modeling Life Fundamentals through Coaching

"Tennis uses the language of life. Advantage, service, fault, break, love—the basic elements of tennis are those of everyday existence, because every match is a life in miniature."
Andre Agassi

Clutching the ball tightly next to his ribs, a juvenile high school football player dashed towards the end zone, plowing past any opponent that dared to confront him. Just before crossing the twenty yard line, his knees gave way as number 24 tackled him to the ground. He felt a distinct cracking sound as the impact force smashed his skull into the plastic abomination that was once his helmet. While he lay motionless on the ground, number 24 showed a smug smirk of satisfaction knowing that the concussion he dealt the opposing team's star player would render him unable to play for the rest of the season. The game continued on with a crushing loss for the star player's team.

As tennis enthusiasts, we are lucky to play and teach a sport in accord with morals and values applicable outside of the sports realm. While football coaches promote ideas of sportsmanship and respect, tennis players can be more actively engaged in displaying these qualities on-court, and hence be well-suited to apply their sportsmanship values to the outside world. It is vital that coaches are able to instill these values into their players to make them not only appreciate the sport more, but also to create more productive members of society.

To preface the importance of teaching these fundamentals, let's start by asking: "What if we don't?" We all have probably witnessed the aftermath of a toxic player's rampage. Whether it be racquets artistically deformed into the shape of a banana, language as colorful as a rainbow, or attempts at breaking Mickey Mantle's legendary home run record, it never ends well. *Never.* Even McEnroe himself, the notoriously short-tempered tennis legend, talks about how much better he could have played if he had only improved his attitude. Not every scenario will be quite as extreme, but promoting moral conduct is important in showing players how to be the best version of themselves and translating positive qualities into their life outside of tennis.

One of the first life fundamentals that coaches should teach is accountability. In an individual sport such as tennis, this aspect is extremely important. There are no teammates, and depending on the match, there probably aren't any referees either. The fact that you are out there all by yourself means that, realistically, there is nobody to blame but yourself. Sure, there's the wind and the court surface, but after placing the blame on Mother Nature, you would hope that players would soon realize how ridiculous they sound. "Oh, the stars didn't align properly and threw my shot off, so I hit my forehand wide."

In the working world, employers always look for potential employees that are able to demonstrate accountability. Nothing is more frustrating than dealing with somebody who constantly makes excuses instead of taking responsibility. Not only are excuses annoying to hear, but even worse, they don't open up any avenues for solutions going forward. Somebody who makes excuses may feel more comfortable with continuing that practice in order to mitigate consequences that keep building up. An accountable person is able to accept guilt and embarrassment that follows after failure to accomplish something, but then uses that as motivation to do it right the next time. Tennis players who are accustomed to accepting responsibility for failure can more easily translate their positive mindset to work and interpersonal relationships to better succeed in life.

Experienced tennis players learn to work under pressure. Tennis has a massive variety of different pressure situations, such as maintaining appropriate shot selection while losing or staying consistent against an offensive player, and tennis players encounter these situations in almost every match. The ability to stay cool and collected not only increases a player's chance of winning, but it helps them stay motivated from start to finish.

Players who work well under pressure are able to think critically. What is the cause of the three unforced errors I hit in a row? And more importantly, how can I fix it? Perhaps one of the most useful aspects of tennis to transfer into work or personal life is a solution-based thought process. If players are unable or unwilling to find solutions, then they rely on somebody else to come up with ideas for improvement. Just like in a match, you're on your own in life. Sure, there are people to guide you to success; however, it is impractical to rely on assistance for any small bump in the road that you may encounter.

Athletes who are able to come up with their own solutions develop a heightened sense of autonomy and possess great leadership qualities. In fact, many people turn to someone that they know is a good-problem solver to inquire advice. People acknowledge independence and confidence, both qualities developed by experienced tennis players, which will make a player more respectable and authoritative as a leader. Through utilizing these attributes, tennis players open up a wide variety of different mentorship possibilities to guide others through life and aid others in any struggles that may arise.

Tennis players develop heart for the game, and are able to utilize their passion to inspire others. One of the most important qualities of a leader is charisma, as it allows players to directly influence others' lives through inspiration. Charismatic people are much more inclined to help others, and the sense of satisfaction gained from helping others spreads to anybody that they come into contact with.

Finally, tennis players learn to take risks. Tennis is a sport where players are always weighing risk versus reward, and they tend to become adept at it. Besides, playing the sport without taking risks just becomes stale. Those that learn to take proper risks end up enjoying tennis more than players who only hit moon balls from the baseline out of fear of making an error. On the flip side, players that take too many risks may become frustrated at themselves, and so it is important for developing players to learn appropriate management of weighing risk and reward. Players who develop this skill are able to translate this into their life through avoiding the monotony of day-in, day-out work and add more flavor to their life.

Coaching encompasses more than the fundamentals of tennis; it works towards creating honest, hard-working individuals. Tennis players can apply ideas such as perseverance, critical thinking, and positive attitude to their life outside of sports to become more productive members of society. Through their heart for the game, players can share their passion and become a role model for others.

What Kind of Mentor Are You?

"Example is not the main thing in influencing others,
it is the only thing."
Albert Schweitzer

Mentorship is a valuable tool for sharing ideas and inspiring others. There is no better feeling than to have a powerful effect on someone's life. Sometimes the best mentoring can occur without either party realizing it's happening. It's the mutually beneficial relationship between mentor and mentee that fosters growth and creates a healthy, learning-based environment.

From the perspective of the mentor, mentorship is a powerful inspirational tool to help others grow. The scope of mentorship is both wide and deep. A mentor has a profound effect on others' lives both inside and outside the workplace. Not only is the mentor's job to help guide persons through their professional lives, but also to be a role model. Actions certainly speak louder than words with mentors. In other words, every single thing mentors do, whether through teaching, body language, or facial communication is noticed and influences by everyone.

With great power and authority comes great responsibility, and this is especially true of mentoring. Although mentors have the ability to influence people positively, it could be counterproductive if mentors do not recognize their role as exemplars and take that role seriously. Being a mentor is an extra duty added to the weight of coach, teacher, and professional and should be viewed as equally important as the other three. It is essential to the mentoring process that mentors act appropriately at all times since mentees will always hold their mentors to the highest of standards. A good mentor will be aware of this and uses it to be a better teacher by using the following list of qualities below:

Approachable and ready to listen. Good mentors take this responsibility seriously. Being approachable means being easily accessible. It means really paying attention when the person you are mentoring is sharing an idea. The mentee is often just as passionate as the mentor and typically has good ideas that should be heard actively.

Accountable for passing along all aspects of the position. As a mentor, it is important to let the mentee know all parts of the job are important. They remember what it was like to be in their situation and make sure that they provide that person with every tool and all the knowledge to be successful.

Always proud of their successes. Every success for the mentee is a success for the mentor. Mentors are a source of inspiration and positivity to others, and expressing happiness can create zealous and hard-working individuals.

Always look to provide opportunities that will challenge them and expand their skill set. Through experience, mentors learn that putting themselves into uncomfortable situations can be beneficial in the long run. Whether it is public speaking, teaching an unfamiliar topic, or a variety of other things, not only does the experience itself challenge them, but the satisfaction of knowing that they can overcome arduous obstacles helps them to become better mentors.

Show the importance of and passion for continuing education. One of the most important qualities of a good mentor is to be ready to learn more and improve each day as a coach. Often, education is necessary for a mentor's own growth, and showing commitment to learning also shows a dedication to helping others how they can improve.

Trustworthy. Mentorship is much more productive if the mentees feel that they are in a comfortable environment to share their feelings and passions. Building trust is an important quality for the mentor and is necessary to create a symbiotic relationship. Mentors need to remember that mentees wants to earn their trust, a task that will reward mentees with a heightened sense of self-confidence.

Show what to do, how to do it, and when to do it. When communicating as a mentor, it's important to remember that keeping a clear and concise message is vital to making sure that one's intended message is not confused. In order to prevent confusion, mentors and coaches need to give precise instructions that contain the what, how, and when.

Constantly ask questions. Mentees who want to succeed as tennis coaches need to audit themselves and understand who they are, where they are in their career, and where they want to be. Questions help mentees be more self-reflective, which inspires them to have a more open mindset. Mentors need to have openness and willingness to help mentees attain their goals.

Clear and confident in their philosophy. Assistant coaches might not always take on your specific coaching philosophy, however, it is very important that they clearly understand coaching progressions they like to follow so they have a roadmap to coach effectively with their own personal style within expected parameters. Finally, the best mentors make sure they provide clear guidance without lecturing.

Take a moment and think of what it would be like to come fresh out of college and want to know what kind of profession to pursue. You are trying to find not just a job, but a specific profession. In some industries, it might not be difficult to find something that works regular hours in the area that you studied. However, in the sports and coaching industry, just finding a place to start can be hard, and this is where having a mentor is a great benefit. Becoming a tennis coach might not be hard, but becoming a successful one is another story altogether. Successful coaches need to make a name for themselves, a brand, and that is not easily done without a solid starting point. Mentors can draw from their own experiences in guiding future coaches through the difficulties they might face, thus opening for them greater opportunities.

Mentors can help create brands for aspiring coaches using their own name and experiences. The first step to becoming successful is to learn how to be successful, and this is a job no better done than by a mentor. Who better to ask how to succeed than somebody who has already become successful? Also, it is certainly beneficial to have an endorsement from someone who has his or her own brand and name, which adds credibility to one's own emerging reputation. Mentors are like a trampoline into the professional world; they provide all of the tools necessary for mentees to give them an extra bounce, but mentee still have to decide to make the jump.

Although mentors can be of great importance in a professional arena, having a tennis coach as a mentor can also be beneficial for those who are still unsure about their career path or even those that aren't looking to go into tennis coaching and management professionally. Mentors provide different elements of inspiration for different people. For those who just play tennis as a hobby or those who play competitively but not professionally, a mentor can be important in finding the right path to follow.

For example, take a look at the world from the perspective of a high-school student who is about to start college. You have absolutely no clue what you want to do with your life, or even how to go about living life after school ends. To have a person other than a friend or family member who is able to provide assistance from a more objective point of view would be a life-saver. Whether it is just basic life skills such as public speaking or advice about personal matters, a mentor is a great asset, especially for somebody who could use the input of another with more life experience.

Mentoring, however, is not the only means of inspiring others or even directly helping others succeed. Mentors can help others develop different real-life skills, including both oral and written communication. Whether it's writing an email or public speaking, mentors have experienced feelings such as fear or nervousness that accompany certain aspects of communicating with others and are able to aid others in overcoming those feelings. Even outside the professional realm, mentors can inspire others to boost their self-confidence in interpersonal relationships and create an increased feeling of self-assurance.

    Mentorship is a powerful tool that can be used to promote learning, encouragement, and growth. It is a mutually beneficial dynamic that is also widely used within the professional realm to animate others to expand their professional vision, but it can also be a valuable tool teaching and motivating those with an intense drive to be successful. Whatever the focus, mentorship is a vital part of both professional and casual life and is an amazingly positive way to help others.

Point 7
Off Court Professionalism

Accessing the Best Continuing Education

"**Leadership and learning are indispensable to each other.**"
John Fitzgerald Kennedy

Continuing education is the lifeblood of any lasting coach's foundation. It allows coaches to grow for the students, the club and themselves. We like to use the following formula – CE (Continuing Education) + PC (Passionate Coach) = CP (Complete Player).

Both of us have been fortunate to take advantage of continuing education workshops at the US Open, Davis Cup Ties, and the BNP Paribas Open on the ways to use high performance coaching in our daily instruction of all people at all levels of play. We have been able to capitalize on those experiences for the betterment of our students and clubs using the LEARN philosophy, which is based on the following principles: **lead, engage, be attentive, recharge, and networking.**

Lead – We have already established that a coach is a student's mentor and leader. Any good leader is always hungry to improve each and every day by gaining continuing knowledge in his/her profession. In addition, this knowledge provides the tools for coaches to train other coaches to better serve their students, their club, and the game.

Engage – One of the best parts of our continuing education workshops have been the exchange of ideas with other top coaches from around the country. Each workshop we attend includes an open exchange of ideas on the main topic we are discussing. Our best new coaching ideas for our students or club always start with us having the confidence to participate in the discussion. We always appreciate the respect that all the top pro coaches involved in leading those discussions demonstrate when we present our thoughts and ideas on the topic for the day.

Be Attentive – While continuing education is a requirement for certified coaches, it should be thought of as more than that. It is easy for coaches to attend conferences to make sure they fulfill their necessary continuing education requirements, but the "complete coaches" know how to use that information to help their students improve. We are always impressed by presenters who take the time to listen actively to all participants. Discussions can range from learning how to teach a certain stroke to explaining clearly a certain situation in tennis, or how to run a tournament effectively or coach a junior team tennis practice. One of the easiest ways to retain students and keep them playing a sport comes from new ideas gained in continuing education.

Recharge – A student's energy is a direct reflection of the coach's energy and enthusiasm. All coaches need to recharge by attending continuing education events to ensure that their excitement for teaching the game is obvious to the student. All sports are constantly changing and tennis is no exception. Coaches need to keep abreast of best athletic techniques for performing, the mental aspects of the game, and new games to help students learn. It is important that coaches are as knowledgeable as possible in all areas of their sport so they can address whatever issue their students want to work on.

Network – Networking is something every professional should do. While networking can be beneficial to a coach's career, it is also important for your student's and your club's growth. Some of our best programs and ideas have come through networking with other coaches. As we have discussed before, spreading enthusiasm for the game is a top priority. Everyone knows the phrase "It takes a village to raise a child." The same is true in tennis. "It takes a village to raise and develop a tennis player." Part of being a complete coach means developing a complete player. Networking helps you create new programs for your club, such as "watercooler" events. Watercooler events represent ways to spread the word about how much fun tennis can be beyond the four walls of your club. People who never play tennis hear about your programs because their buddies at work had a great time and can't stop talking about it. This kind of networking allows coaches to tweak already existing programs so they are fun and creative and tailored to the environment of your club and the interests of your members.

Partnering with Peers—Sharing Best Practices

"You'll hear a lot of applause in your life, but none will mean more to you than that applause from your peers."
Andre Agassi

Partnering with Peers—Sharing Best Practices is one of the most important features of effective Off Court Professionals. This book is a perfect example of that philosophy since it is an embodiment of our shared desire to collaborate as coaches, thus serving our students and the industry we both love so much. We agree with this quote from legendary coach Vince Lombardi, "Individual commitment to a group effort—that is what makes a team work, a company work, a society work, and a civilization work."

Tennis for us has always been about believing that everyone with a passion for the game has something to contribute to making the game better and helping it flourish. This belief comes from our experiences of playing on college tennis teams and partnering with our teammates to make our teams the best they can be. So during our time as coworkers, we have always sought to produce the best programs possible. We continue to do so working for different organizations now but still partnering on this book and other projects to serve the game of tennis.

Before we introduce some practices we've found helpful to our professional growth by partnering with peers, we think it is important to ask several questions including the following: Who are your peers? What practices are you looking to improve? While other questions might arise as coaches go through this process we believe that these are the primary ones coaches should use to evaluate and explore how to do great things through teamwork. As we have journeyed through this process of partnership, we have found having similar views on these questions has been vital in helping us grow not only as coaches but as mentors and leaders in tennis. We have found that the following main approaches have been key to our sharing best practices with our peers. These include creating a network of peers and doing cooperative presentations and articles on mutual interests.

Creating a Network of Peers

We believe teamwork among coaches in the industry is the best way to grow and promote the game. Steve Jobs, American entrepreneur, business magnate, inventor, industrial designer and former CEO and co-founder of Apple Inc. once said, "Great things in business are never done by one person. They're done by a team of people." We believe that this quotation can be applied to all coaches working together in teams to do great things for tennis and all those who play the game.

Who are your peers? While coaches have to answer this question for themselves, we believe peers are those who are committed to growing the game and their community through tennis while working collegially with others. Through our years of coaching, we have found that our strongest networks of coaching peers are bound by a passion to make tennis and their communities stronger. This can be done in several ways. It can include setting up annual High School Coaches' workshops, professional continuing education workshops at Pro Tournaments such as Citi Open in Washington D.C. or fundraisers for a charity cause including one for Breast Cancer Research called "Swing for Pink." Many of our best ideas for classes, programs or lessons have come from the shared exchange of ideas from these workshops. These ideas can emerge through simple presentations where participants just exchange "drill or program ideas." This approach has helped us develop a network of peers not just in our immediate area but nationwide and internationally. These kinds of events have helped us to create, sustain and grow our network of peers looking to improve the game of tennis and their community.

Doing Cooperative Presentations & Articles of Mutual Interest

One thing we are sure of is this—cooperation equals creativity and confidence for a coach. We have to admit we are "tennis nuts." We love talking about all aspects of tennis—history, the mental game, the best drill concepts and many other topics. We have frequently done on court drill sessions with each other during down times between lessons to learn from each other. This passion for always wanting to know how to pass along our love for the game to others is what drives us each day.

The roots of this book revolve around our desire to challenge ourselves to communicate topics through cooperative projects that inspire other coaches and people in our industry. We have found that great coaches use the attitude "spreading tennis is my business and it can be done with people beyond the four walls of your club or organization." In other words, we want to encourage coaches to "think outside the box." Below are the ten ways that have been helpful to us in achieving this important goal of working together for the good of tennis. In every case they

- Identify our Guiding Principles as Coaches
- Provide Awareness of our Strengths and Weaknesses as Coaches
- Help Us Know our Specific Passions as Coaches
- Improve our Communication Skills
- Allow us to be More Thoughtful with our Coaching Intentions
- Help us Learn from Other Coaches
- Provide an Avenue for Spreading our Knowledge
- Build Confidence
- Keep Us Recharged Off the Court
- Keep us Motivated

You want to grow the game of tennis? Then grow your network of peers and share best practices with each other. Tennis is an ever-changing sport, and it is vital that coaches work together to better serve their students and the game.

Solutions for Teaching Pro Challenges

"Don't find fault, find a remedy."
Henry Ford

"Successful leaders see the opportunities in every difficulty rather than the difficulty in every opportunity."
Reed Markham

While coaching is certainly a most rewarding profession, it also can be very challenging. Coaches often feel overworked and underappreciated. Monthly budgets can be difficult. Sometimes coaches are presented with unclear professional paths. Sometimes they find it hard to carve out time to participate in continuing education. Some cultures do not promote a team environment. Just as in any profession, coaching has its times of trial and testing, we believe there are solutions that we have found to be helpful if you stay committed to them.

Below are issues that face the coaching profession and solutions to help with each challenge:

Challenge: Having the Feeling of Being Overworked and Underappreciated
Solution: This is one of the biggest reasons tennis coaches leave the profession or their club. One of the most powerful tools a tennis coach has is serving as a source of inspiration for students to learn in a fun, cooperative environment away from the everyday stresses of life. Any student's energy on court will be a reflection of the coach's energy toward teaching that student and wanting that student to enjoy his/her time on the court.

Below are easy and effective ways to help foster an environment of appreciation for a coach:

- If students take the time to tell you as the Tennis Director that they really enjoyed their lessons with one of your coaches, make sure you tell the coach responsible for the lessons personally as soon as possible to show that you appreciate how that coach helped those students enjoy their tennis experience.
- If you see a teaching technique done by a coach that is new and really helps a student, congratulate the pro on taking the time to come up with a creative teaching solution to help that particular student.
- As Tennis Director or Head Pro ensure you are consistent with all your coaches regarding any coaching, scheduling or other tennis department policies.
- Ensure that any coaching and professional development success by a coach is passed along as a success to club/organization members. This will let the coach know that you value the extra commitment he/she took to expanding his/her knowledge of the game for his/her students.
- It is important in setting coaching team schedules to achieve a healthy work/life balance for your coaches.

Challenge: Sometimes It's Hard to Set a Personal Monthly Budget

Solution: This is probably one of the greatest challenges for coaches. First and foremost coaches should have a personal goal each month that identifies all types of lessons—privates, small group privates, and clinics. We have found that knowing exactly how many of these different types of lessons a coach is looking to teach each month allows for better planning. This method also forces a coach to plan a development path for his/her players. It is imperative that when setting these goals coaches think about an ACE method. First the goals should be "attainable" based on such factors as existing and potential clientele and court availability. Second they must be "clear" to the coach and the club. Clear here means providing exact revenue figures or number of lessons each week or month. Finally, they should be "efficient." They should be able to be achieved within a schedule that allows coaches to perform at 100% for each lesson. By finding a way to plan a consistent budget coaches will ensure their financial security and also the club's financial stability.

Challenge: Unclear Professional Path

Solution: Upward mobility is important in any profession. It is important that Directors and clubs are clear to their coaches on what leads to upward mobility. This can include the number of new members recruited for the club, lesson revenues, the amount of continuing education completed, accreditation upgrades, or the number of players recruited for clinics. Each position within the club's tennis department must clearly show the expectations for upward mobility. In addition, every tennis position should include some aspect of ownership for coaches allowing them to take the lead in new ideas or programs.

Challenge: Finding Time or Resources to Participate in Continuing Education

Solution: Our involvement in continuing education is by far the most important off court activity we have done. As mentioned earlier, it has provided us with many incredible opportunities including learning from pro coaches at workshops held during major pro events such as the US Open and Indian Wells BNP Paribas. Participating in continuing education demonstrates commitment, helps with creativity and builds confidence. While finding time or resources to participate can sometimes be a challenge, it is essential that coaches commit to this part of their professional development. As we have discussed previously, being competent and creative are the benchmarks of any great coach. These two qualities are directly derived from continued learning.

Below are ways to find time or resources to participate in continuing education:

- It starts with making commitments to attend a certain amount of continuing education each year and communicating that to the club and/or Tennis Director
- Tennis Directors can help their coaches achieve continuing education by ensuring rotations of coaches attending conferences/workshops during the year
- In order to help coaches attend workshops financially, tennis directors need to provide incentives such as signup goals for classes that when achieved will have the club pay for all or part of the expense of workshops and any travel involved
- Encourage coaches during downtime at the club to watch online continuing education webinars

Challenge: Some Institutions do not provide a Team Environment

Solution: In tennis, individual accountability, individual determination and teamwork can be taught. If you are playing on a high school team, a college team, Davis Cup Team, Federation Cup Team, or a USTA League Team both individual and team values are important. This is something that we have learned through our years of coaching.

While coaches are always working to build their brand, we have found that coaches are most inspired and productive when team building incentives are set in place. For example, make coaches aware of sign up or revenue goals the club has and tie a fun incentive to them. If such goals are met, then take the coaches out for dinner or a fun event at the end of each month. If you want your players to function as a team, your coaches need to model teamwork with each other. While as with any industry coaches face many challenges, there are always solutions that can help prevent them from leaving the profession while at the same time thriving and enjoying it!

Match Point

The End Game

"Success is a journey, not a destination.
The doing is usually more important than the outcome."
Arthur Ashe

"We make a living by what we get,
but we make a life by what we give."
Winston Churchill

As tennis players, coaches, and enthusiasts, we certainly understand the inspiring feeling of victory, and this book is dedicated to helping *you* win in coaching and in life. Just like a tennis match, creating those victories takes practice and dedication, two concepts which cannot be adhered to without others to guide you. Through our experiences as coaches, finding mentors and being surrounded by an intellectual community dedicated to improving the lives of others have become the biggest sources of inspiration to continue in the coaching profession.

One of the most important aspects of coaching is that it is about the journey, not the destination. The destination always changes, and focusing solely on where you end up will leave you puzzled and disoriented when an injury finds you unable to coach, or certain bureaucratic paperwork prevents you from taking advantage of a particular opportunity. Instead, stay focused on growing as a person, and take those skills and use them to inspire others. Tim certainly can attest to this philosophy as adaptation is what led him to success despite living in a foreign country.

Developing a coaching philosophy and adhering to it has helped us succeed as coaches. Coaching as a profession is all about branding and creating a fresh identity that is easily recognizable by others. Creating a brand has helped us as coaches to become better-known and more successful, and the steps to marketing yourself start with your own self-reflection.

In light of this observation, what legacy will you leave the world? It doesn't need to be big; it just needs to be meaningful. Whether it's fostering the growth of others through learning tennis, inspiring others by way of example, or becoming a mentor to guide people through their professional or personal lives, enjoy the ride and the impact that you are making on the world!

Final Thoughts

Our goal in this book has been to answer the question "What is the Complete Coach?" We have attempted to help you solve the coaching puzzle, but you still have to put the pieces together for yourself. We can't do that for you. While we laid out the principles, philosophies, and guidelines that we believe will help every tennis coach and coaches in general, we also hope that this book will encourage you to be more confident in your own philosophy as a coach.
      The greatest gift a coach can give is the ability to influence the lives of others positively—mentally, physically, emotionally, and socially, regardless of age, gender or background. We hope that you are ready now to go out and serve your students and collaborate with your fellow coaches in a way that you have never done before!

Made in the USA
Middletown, DE
20 January 2018